FAR HORIZONS

FAR HORIZONS

Adventure travel for all - where to go and what to do

**by
Walt Unsworth**

CICERONE PRESS
MILNTHORPE, CUMBRIA, U.K.

ISBN 1 85284 228 8
A catalogue record of this book is available from the British Library

*To the memory of Patrick Hurley,
companion on many an adventure*

Acknowledgements

My thanks are due to the many adventure travel companies, airlines and tourist
offices with whom I have worked over the years and without whom this book
would not have been possible. A special word of thanks must go to Steve
Newman for his invaluable help and to my wife Dorothy for her background
support and assistance during my travels.

Walt Unsworth, Cumbria, 1997

The colour content of this book has been generously supported by Explore Worldwide Ltd, a
leading adventure travel company. Cicerone is grateful to Travers Cox and Explore Worldwide
for their support.

Cover picture: *View from the South Rim, Grand Canyon*
Frontispiece: *Thyangboche Monastery, Nepal (Ch 2)*

CONTENTS

LIST OF COLOUR ILLUSTRATIONS

Illustrated throughout by the author

INTRODUCTION
You too can have an adventure

"Something hidden. Go and find it. Go and look behind the Ranges -
Something lost behind the Ranges. Lost and waiting for you. Go!"

Kipling

If you have glanced at any of the glossy brochures stacked on the racks of your local travel agent you could be forgiven for thinking that nothing much has changed in the holiday business in the last twenty years. The same old promises of sun, sea and sand; hotels and chalets on the beach or, for the more cultural holiday, a visit to Venice, or Prague, or Vienna, or perhaps all three. But then, if you look through the travel sections of the weekend papers you can see a different kind of holiday of a sort most high street travel agents don't carry - adverts promising adventure in strange countries with deserts and canyons, high mountains and bleak moors. This is known as 'adventure travel' and is one of the fastest growing sectors of the holiday business.

The simple fact is that most people these days do not need a rest, they need a change. Holidays just lying around are boring - much better to be up and doing. But doing what? Well, there are activity holidays where you can learn ballooning or climbing or a multitude of other sports, but they are rather specialised things which don't concern us here. What most people go for is travel which has an element of adventure, a touch of the unknown with a frisson of excitement.

The adventure could be a mild one, such as following some well-marked trail like a French Grande Randonnée or it could be something tough and quite dangerous, like thrashing through the Borneo jungle or rafting down the Colorado. Whatever it is, the chances are that you will come back with memorable experiences, maybe even the adventures of a lifetime. I remember once meeting an elderly chap in a Delhi restaurant who had just returned from a Himalayan trek and was glowing with pride. "This is my sixth year of adventure," he declared. "I spent forty years in a factory and when I retired I thought of all the things I'd never done and all the places I'd never seen and I determined to make up for it. Now I've spent all my savings, and I don't regret a penny of it!"

There is a lot in the saying that you are as young as you feel and age is no barrier to adventure for anyone who is moderately fit. After all, even Everest has been climbed by men well over 50. A friend of mine did the thousand mile walk called the Way of St James from Le Puy in France to Compostella in Spain when he was 66. A recent survey by a leading adventure travel company has shown that 59% of customers were over 35, with the average age being 41. Half travelled alone, and 56% were women.

Then there was Max, with whom I travelled through the jungles of Sarawak. Max was in his thirties and saved every penny so that he could go on *two* trips a year - one mountaineering (he had climbed Aconcagua, Kilimanjaro, Elbruz and Kinabalu) and one general adventure.

Most of us are less ambitious than these but would like to try at least one adventure. This book tells you what is involved in the many options now available for the ordinary person who spends most of the year behind an office desk or at a lathe. We can't all be Chris Boningtons or Blashford Snells but this book shows we don't need to be. The choice is so wide that in the immortal words of TV's Arthur Daley, "The world is your lobster!"

Perhaps by this time next year you will have stood on the summit of Africa's highest peak, crossed the Grand Canyon from rim to rim, or discovered the lost roads of the Etruscans. One of the greatest of British explorers, Bill Tilman, was once asked what was needed for an expedition. "Just put your boots on and go," he replied.

The question is, where to go and who to go with? In the following chapters there are lots of examples of the sorts of places you can visit and hopefully these will inspire you but the question of who to go with is not an easy one to answer. The adventure travel companies are not all alike, by any means. Some embrace a wide range of holidays in many parts of the world, and others tend to concentrate on one or two areas. There are also firms offering only special interest journeys for birdwatching, exploring battlefields etc. (see Appendix 1). Some of the bigger firms offer tours of all sorts from cross desert vehicle journeys to tramping and camping in Iceland, or sailing round the Galapagos. Others concentrate entirely on walking tours.

Many travellers choose a company on the recommendation of a friend, and there is a high degree of brand loyalty, with travellers choosing the same firm time and again. Some companies have a travelling road show in which they give lectures and slide shows about their journeys when you can not only see what is on offer but meet people who have perhaps been on some of the trips. Another way of finding out is to join one of the several "travel clubs" recently established (see Appendix 3).

But in the end it comes down to choosing from the brochures and it is worth your while to study several. The companies likely to be of interest you can glean from the adverts in the Sunday papers, or in some of the adventure magazines (see Appendix 3), or more comprehensively by getting the AITO

Directory (see Appendix 1). It will become apparent quite quickly that prices and services vary widely, even for the same area, but there are usually good reasons. Things to look out for and weigh up include such points as: is it a camping trip, hotel based, or a mixture? is it backpacking or luggage assisted, that is, the heavy luggage carried by porters or sent on ahead by vehicle? is it guided throughout or are you given a map and expected to fend for yourself? are flights included in the price - sometimes they are not? are all meals included or is there a 'kitty'? how much are single supplements? what are the maximum and minimum numbers on the tour? does the company specialise in certain groups, such as SAGA does for the over-50s, or Uranian Travel for gays?

Any company should be prepared to answer your doubts and queries and may even send you a more detailed itinerary of any trip you are considering. Further details will certainly be forthcoming after a booking is made. It should give all the practical details you need to know about visas, currency and kit, though in my experience they are a little tardy on the medical side. Some companies, too, it must be said, leave tickets and visas to the last minute.

It is essential to have a medical and dental check-up before you go off into the blue, and to seek the latest medical advice about malaria (different areas require different tablets) and inoculations if your trip requires these precautions. For remote tropical areas it is worth contacting MASTA (0891 224 100) who will supply detailed instructions about all your medical needs based on your itinerary. Specific hazards travellers meet with are dealt with in various appropriate chapters of the book, though tummy troubles are so common it was difficult to know which chapter to put it in. (it ended up in Ch 3 eventually!).

You need to sort out the currency in advance too. Adventure travel often takes place in Third World countries where the currency is nothing like as stable as our own - it can go up and down like a yo-yo. If you have any left over at the end of the trip you will probably not be allowed to take it out of the country - and if you did nobody would change it! The trick is to try and balance the cash you need whilst you are there - and *cash* you certainly will need for not all countries accept credit cards, or even travellers' cheques. In China, for example, only certain banks in a town are allowed to cash travellers' cheques and the chances are these will be either closed when you visit them, or will have run out of the appropriate forms. Except for destinations which have their own hard currency, travellers' cheques should be in US dollars, a currency universally understood. Credit cards are more problematical - sophisticated places such as Singapore or Hong Kong will take credit cards like a shot, but it can be a problem in many other places. But you never know - I once sat cross-legged in a bazaar in Leh in remote Ladakh bargaining for a *thanka*, a sort of religious wall hanging, only to find that I did not have enough cash. Much to my surprise out came the machine and the deal was done through AMEX. That'll do nicely! But don't rely on it. Incidentally, cards are useful at airports if you are just passing through and don't have the local currency - I have purchased small items such as a comb (Los Angeles) and a cup of coffee (Singapore) using a card.

Ironical that I should be passing through LA airport and not have any dollars, but I was travelling to New Zealand which is a hard currency area and so didn't need them. Normally American dollars are the cash to carry. They are universally exchangeable for local currency and you will often get a good price for them on the open market, though you should beware of any currency regulations. Your local guide will often act as broker, or will know a man who does!

It is useful to have some local currency to start with because there are times when you are whisked off almost immediately from the airport to some remote destination without a chance to change money and it can be hard to catch up. When ordering the money insist on small notes. Banks always like to dish out huge bank-notes if they can, but in remote areas it is difficult to get a large note changed - it probably represents the shopkeeper's normal monthly income.

Although I have been on quite a number of adventure holidays I still worry about what kit to take. The basics are easy enough and I have made out a list in Appendix 4, but I always feel there is something I should have included but didn't, or vice-versa. Every trip is different, and you learn something about packing from every one.

So much depends on where you are going. Obviously the gear you need for Arabia is not the same as you need for Greenland, but there are subtle differences too - hot dry conditions like Grand Canyon may be made more bearable by T-shirts which breathe and wick away the sweat, whereas in hot wet conditions, like climbing Kinabalu on Borneo, you'd be wasting your time, because you are going to get soaking wet no matter what you wear and an ordinary thin cotton T-shirt is best. Horses for courses. For general wear there is nowadays some excellent travel gear, stuff which will take a hammering and still come up looking reasonable. The pioneer in this was Rohan, whose trousers, known as Bags, are legendary. They can be wet through yet dry in a trice, roll up very small for packing, and have umpteen pockets, several zipped, which frustrates pick-pockets like nothing else I know. A would-be pick-pocket in Cuzco, Peru, gave up in disgust with my Bags some years ago and ran off as I was about to collar him. There is a whole range of Rohan gear, and several other makes of a similar type nowadays.

Shorts are a popular option but if you wear shorts remember to put plenty of sun block on your legs - years ago I suffered so badly for neglecting this on Kilimanjaro that I have never made the same mistake again. On the other hand because the weather can change very quickly in the mountains walkers who wear shorts should always carry a pair of long trousers in the day sack. It would be deep irony to get sunburn and hypothermia on the same day! It could happen.

Just as you need a sun hat and T-shirts for a hot clime so you need thermal underwear and balaclava for a cold clime, but no matter how hot or cold you expect it to be always take a sample of the alternative. Even in the tropics a sweater sometimes comes in handy and glaciers, which you might expect to be cold, are extremely hot from the sun's glare. You can start the morning hike in duvet jacket and balaclava and by noon be in T-shirt and sun hat. An experienced traveller always expects the unexpected.

For temperate climes and even hot climes clothing is not too difficult, but where severe cold is expected it can be a problem ie. at high altitudes, or in the Arctic or Antarctic regions or in winter. Thermal underwear, a duvet jacket or even, for high altitudes or extreme cold, a duvet suit, three sets of gloves - inner, outer and mitts, double boots, wool shirts... all very expensive. If you are thinking of joining one of the high altitude expeditions now available to adventure travellers your gear is going to cost at least £500 and perhaps much more. But then, if you are going to join a high altitude expedition, you will be experienced enough to know that.

The universal footwear for travellers these days is the trainer, though recently the sports sandal has gained fashion. Even some of the long distance walks can be done in trainers - I remember doing the Loue-Lison walk in France and the Abel Tasman Coastal Walk in New Zealand this way - but for anything more strenuous lightweight walking boots are better. I have used Brasher boots for many years and find them very comfortable. For high altitudes involving snow, a stiffer soled boot which will take a crampon might be necessary.

Most of the gear listed in Appendix 4 is self evident and I offer it chiefly as an *aide-mémoire* for when you come to pack. Heavier gear like tents and cooking materials will be provided by the travel company, though if you are camping you will need your own sleeping bags, inner and outer. Once again, the quality of the bag will depend on the temperatures expected and for cold conditions a 'four-seasons' bag is the minimum required. Utensils are generally supplied but it is always useful to have your own mug, knife, fork and spoon. The mug should be plastic and marked with your initials. And a useful tip for Eastern bound travellers - learn how to use chopsticks!

For carrying purposes you need three items (1) a large hold-all, kitbag or rucksack, to carry your bulk luggage (2) a day sack for everyday use (3) a bum-bag to hold personal items.

Old fashioned kitbags or stuff-bags were popular with trekkers at one time, but they have given way to the large hold-all, or grip, in which the gear is more readily accessible through the long zip. It needs to be of tough material able to withstand the rigours of adventure travel, where it will be chucked onto trucks, flung over the backs of yaks or perched on the head of a porter. Some travel companies supply them as part of the deal. But do you need a grip or a rucksack? Sometimes it is difficult to decide and to overcome that

On assisted walking tours vehicles are used to transport the heavy gear from place to place allowing the walker the freedom of carrying a light day sack

problem there are combination bags like the Karrimor Sequoia which can be converted from a bag to a rucksack as necessary. It also has a small - very small - day sack built in. The Sequoia is 75 litres capacity, which is about right for a trekking pack. It is as tough as old boots, though fairly expensive and heavy.

Whatever you use, never assume that it is waterproof, despite what the makers say. A tropical downpour in the jungles of Borneo or South America will soak anything. The answer lies in plastic bags - the sort you get free at a supermarket. Pack everything in plastic bags and have a few spare. They not only keeps clothes dry but can be used for sorting dirty washing.

Your day sack also needs protection and the best thing is a bin liner, because everything is then easily accessible. This is the sack you carry yourself. In it go your immediate needs - waterproofs, toilet paper, emergency kit like plasters, first aid items, torch and map and compass - depending, as ever, on where you are and what you are doing. Your waterbottle and lunch go in it too, and fastidious people may even carry washing kit! It is also the best place to keep a camera out of harm's way unless you are carrying a special camera bag (see Appendix 2). A rucksack of 25/30 litres is about right. Some travellers prefer the day sack to have side pockets because of the ready access they give to items in constant use, like the waterbottle, and recently I was tempted into getting one; but it is hard to teach an old dog new tricks and after a couple of journeys I reverted to my old familiar Hot Ice, a Karrimor sack designed for winter climbing which I have had since the days when I indulged in such mad activities! No external pockets, but very comfortable.

Porters on Kinabalu, Borneo

Bum-bags are more controversial. There is no doubt that they are vulnerable to theft and should not be flaunted, but discreetly hidden under T-shirt, sweater or whatever and kept with the bag round the front - a tum-bag rather than a bum-bag. Nevertheless it is useful if only to keep spare film, sun block, bites cream and passport in. You may prefer a money belt, hidden beneath your shirt for money and credit cards, or one of the many pockets of your Rohans. Not wise to put all your eggs in one bum-bag! But by spreading your valuables around, as indicated, you should be safe and at least won't lose everything at once.

Trekking poles have gained immensely in popularity over the last few years. These look like collapsible ski-sticks, with a basket at one end and a handle at the other. The proper way to use them is in pairs, getting up a swinging rhythm, something like a langlauf skier. It makes load carrying uphill that much easier - but in the adventure travel situation it is only the harder treks where this is necessary. Nevertheless, a single pole is of value, especially going downhill. In the last two or three years I have become a convert to poles though I have discovered that if they are gripped too tightly throughout the day you can end up with the equivalent of tennis-elbow. This is very painful. It can be avoided by holding the pole loosely and using the handle strap to take the strain. A friend of mine is designing some revolutionary

15

orthopaedic poles which he reckons will do away with this, but we must wait and see.

Improvements to gear come along from time to time to make life easier for the adventure traveller, but gear in itself is not important - only what it achieves. There are not many gear-freaks in this activity anyway. Things of the spirit are more important; after all, you don't go to Machu Picchu to try out a new rucksack. It is the journey that matters, and when you think about it, life is one long journey. The poet Christina Rossetti put it like this:

> *Does the road wind uphill all the way?*
> *Yes, to the very end.*
> *Will the day's journey take the whole long day?*
> *From morn to night, my friend.*

The Golo valley in Corsica offers a splendid day's walk, sampling the famous GR20 (Ch 1)

Yosemite Valley, California, seen from Glacier Point. This beautiful valley has many fine walks (Ch 1)

One of the most exciting walks in Yosemite is the Mist Trail, so called because of the spray from the Vernal Falls (Ch 1)

In a valley near Sovana, Tuscany. Following the ancient Etruscan roads to Orvieto makes an interesting expedition (Ch 1)

The Abel Tasman Coast Track on New Zealand's South Island passes many fine beaches like this at Onetahuti (Ch 1)

The superb southern face of Mont Blanc seen from the Torino Hut. The hut is easily reached by cable-car from the route of the TMB (Ch 2)

The trek up the Khumbu valley to Everest reveals a succession of memorable views including this of the Kangtega group seen from the Pheriche Pass (Ch 2)

Clouds gather over the ruins of Machu Picchu, the 'lost city of the Incas' and culmination of the Inca Trail in Peru (Ch 2)

Steadiness and stamina are required for an ascent of Angels Landing in Zion Canyon, Utah. The final peak, shown here, is climbed with the aid of fixed chains (Ch 2)

Walkers on the Via delle Bocchette, Brenta Dolomites, Italy. This exciting via ferrata is justifiably one of the most popular 'iron roads' (Ch 2)

1
Tracks and Trails

L et's start our adventures with a look at the simplest and easiest kind of holiday - the walking tour. Travelling on foot is sometimes the only way a place can be reached. In the following chapters, most, if not all, the gorges, mountains and jungles described cannot be reached by any other way. There's a closeness to nature that no other method of travelling can achieve - only a walker can see the giant mop-headed rhododendrons on Kinabalu or the Col de la Vanoise covered in a blue carpet of gentians. Only a walker can hear the whistle of a marmot warning its mates or swing over a raging Himalayan river on a rope bridge. Sometimes there's a closeness to nature which is a little too close for comfort - but in that lies the adventure!

The level of fitness required to undertake a walking tour is not as great as many imagine. It is well within the capabilities of the average man or woman. In any case, all the companies who run these tours grade them in the brochure according to how strenuous they are, taking into account length of walks, roughness of terrain, exposure and altitude. You pays your money and takes your choice, and if you are not accustomed to walking you'd be wise to tackle something easier to start with. The problem here is that there is no consistency between tour operators, and sometimes 'easy' means very easy, perhaps disappointingly so, whereas in other instances 'easy' means reasonable. But combined with the descriptions in the brochure and perhaps some guidebooks, you should be able to make an intelligent guess as to what you are letting yourself in for.

Even so, it would be foolish to imagine that you can lead a sedentary life for fifty weeks of the year and then dash off and do the Tour of Mont Blanc. The first few days would be very tiring and you'd probably feel like giving up. Some preliminary exercise is required - and the best exercise for walking is to walk! A day out on the local moors once a month is enough to get you in shape. If you are not accustomed to walking then build up your performance over the months. Start with five miles of gentle stroll, then add some ups and downs and build up to fifteen miles. You should manage this by your fourth or fifth walk and if you do it regularly - not necessarily very frequently - you should be able to manage most of the tours in the brochures.

Of equal importance to physical fitness is mental fitness. It is essential to be mentally tuned to the tour you are doing and have the mental reserves necessary to carry it through. A bit of determination goes a long way.

Walking holidays can be divided into two broad kinds. In the first kind, the walking is in interesting country, along tracks and trails which though they may be rough going at times are intrinsically straightforward in that there are no technical problems to worry about and particularly no problems of altitude or exposure. The second kind involves high mountains with the possibility of mountain sickness and hypothermia, or rocky terrain that involves scrambling along exposed ridges and ledges. Or perhaps the technical problems of jungle bashing. In other words, harsh uncompromising terrain which could be life-threatening. In this chapter I intend to deal with the first kind: the walking tour without extremes.

Trying to analyse my own experience of this kind of trip, I find it falls into one of three categories: the fixed centre holiday, the ride-and-walk holiday and the trail or trek type. These are largely self explanatory. The fixed centre is based in a single hotel or camp and day walks are done from there, returning to base each evening; the second is really an extension of the first except that you move base from time to time and do day walks from a variety of centres; whilst the third sort means you move on each day, on foot, usually following a specific trail like King Ludwig's Way in Bavaria, or the Long Trail in America - there are dozens of them.

A walking holiday based on a single centre is particularly suited to Europe, where there is a long tradition of such holidays and plenty of hotels catering for them. It is the simplest form of all adventure holidays and can quite easily be organised off your own bat, without help from anybody. After all, there's no hassle about visas or jabs, no complicated travel - indeed, with the Channel Tunnel now available you may even be able to drive straight there from your own front door.

Doing it on your own there's all the excitement of discovery. Armed with a map and possibly a guidebook, you can explore the local walks, some of which will be gems. Alas, some will be dross, and this is where the guided holiday scores. The guide will know (or should know!) the best walks. The guide can also judge the capabilities of the party and bear this in mind when choosing the routes. A good guide will actually push you to the limit, but not over it.

Throughout Europe there are many villages and hamlets which can provide good walking; places in the Vosges, the Jura, the Dolomites, the Apennines, in Norway, and practically the whole of Austria. Companies such as Waymark, Ramblers, and Headwater specialise in this sort of trip. Many of the islands mentioned in Ch 6 are ideal for centre based walking. Here is a typical day walk my wife and I did recently in Corsica.

A Corsican Valley

The island of Corsica rises out of the Mediterranean in a series of spiky granite ridges separated by deep, lush valleys. It is incredibly beautiful and it lends itself to walking. One of the long-distance walks here, the GR20, Corsican High Level Route is reputed to be the hardest walk of its kind in Europe but the island also has much to offer the less ambitious. From a centre like Evisa, north of Ajaccio, it is possible to do a variety of day walks, albeit with the aid of a car to reach the starting points.

One of the best of these walks is that up the Golo Valley towards the fine peaks of Tafunatu and Paglia Orba. The walk coincides in part with the GR20, so you are able to get at least a taste of that famous route. Like all good walks there are times when it is rough and times when it is tough, but mostly it is just staggeringly beautiful.

It was a warm May morning when, with three companions, I set off from the Col de Verghio into the Golo Valley. Our leader was Sarah, one of the guides employed by Jean Angelini, a dynamic Corsican who knows more about his home hills than most and played a large part in establishing the High Route. The col is a watershed between west and east and is marked by a huge statue of Christ standing on a beehive shaped base. We parked the car here and set off along a good path into the valley.

Soon we were travelling through a splendid silver birch plantation and then, as we dipped towards a side stream, the birch gave way to Corsican pines. Beyond the trees the route became steadily rockier and granite stones crunched beneath our boots until, crossing a ridge, we came upon the little stone huts of the Bergerie de Radule, their thick low walls sheltered by enormous boulders, tucked beside a tumbling stream. What a situation those huts enjoy! A perfect picture of rocks and trees and rushing waters. These *bergeries* of Corsica are quite common and are the same as the *cheseries* of the Alps; shepherds' huts where cheese is made.

After Radule we directed our attention to the rocky bed of the River Golo which we had to cross. The Golo is a wide and powerful stream and though the water was fairly low, we found the crossing tricky all the same, for it still came splashing down with some force. It was a nervy, teetery business and we were glad to reach the opposite bank. Judge our dismay then, when just a short distance up the valley we had to cross back to the other bank! Fortunately we discovered a flat bedrock that the stream slid over more gently and using this we were able to leap from one bank to the other.

Now we were on a good path again. The sides of the valley rose steeply on either hand and at the valley head we could see the peaks of Tafunatu and Paglia Orba, separated by a broad saddle. Neither looked very impressive. Tafunatu resembled a huge decayed molar but the other, 200m higher, was more solidly constructed, all bold buttresses of pink granite. There is a hole right through Tafunatu but we couldn't make it out from this distance.

In the cirque at the valley head we sat by the stream and ate lunch. Another bergerie, Tula, smaller and meaner than Radule, lay close by and up above, at the head of a steep scree slope, we could just see the small mountain refuge which rejoices in the impressive name of Ciottulu di i Mori.

Above our resting place the side of the valley was a steep slope of grass topped by some rocks and a distinctive ridge. The GR20 went that way, along the ridge to the hut, and Sarah and I decided to climb it whilst the others finished their meal. So up we went, easier than expected, to be greeted by extensive views over the mountains to the west - waves of blue peaks rolling away to the sea. The ridge itself was a walkers' delight and before long we reached the hut where a horde of walkers were scattered about like penguins on an icefloe, all eating lunch. Where they came from I have no idea - perhaps they were all doing the High Level Route! Above the hut the Tafunatu and Paglia Orba rose in rocky splendour.

We slithered down steep broken slopes with an abominable track, which needed care to avoid a twisted ankle or worse, in order to rejoin our companions. We had been away for almost two hours, so they were anxious to be starting back though none of us was looking forward to those tricky stream crossings. Sarah, however, had an idea. She remembered that there was supposed to be a path which stayed on our side of the stream, but it was said to be a difficult one, needing great care. We seized on it eagerly - anything to avoid the rushing waters of the Golo.

We followed the valley down until our way seemed blocked by the rocks of the Capu di a Marla, the buttresses of which acted as a sentinel to the valley entrance. This is where the path swerved aside to cross the river, but sure enough, as we hoped, a narrow ribbon led off towards the peak. Soon it became difficult and exposed, following narrow ledges and crossing very steep slopes. Hands were brought into play as we scrambled across a rocky corner or descended a broken chimney-crack to a lower path. It was fascinating work, slow, cautious, nervy; I think we were all glad when we saw the familiar roofs of the Radule bergerie below us. The scrambling had not really been difficult but looking back, up the cliff we had just descended, we couldn't see any trace of our route. It just seemed impossible.

Any doubts we may have had vanished. Fresh vigour swept into tired limbs. In no time at all we were travelling through the woods back to the Col de Verghio, the car, and a beer in Evisa. It had been a very satisfactory day's walk.

Travelling from place to place by vehicle, sampling walks en route, allows you to cover a wide area on a very selective basis. It works very well in the western United States where the distances are vast and the scenery so varied.

In Bryce Canyon, Utah. The canyon offers short walks in spectacular scenery, amid sandstone towers known as 'hoodoos'

One of the best tours of this sort I ever did was organised through Explore Worldwide. It began and ended in Los Angeles, and its ultimate aim was a crossing of the Grand Canyon on foot (see Ch 7). Our leader Jeff built up to this climax with a series of walks beginning with a stroll along Venice Beach in Los Angeles, followed in succeeding days by the coast near Santa Barbara, Twin Peaks (really!), the Golden Gate Bridge (that's a walk with a difference!), Zabriski Point in Death Valley, Zion's Angels Landing (see Ch 2) and Virgin Narrows (see Ch 7), Cedar Breaks, Ashdown Gorge Wilderness with its Twisted Forest Trail and incredibly ancient bristlecone pines and Brian Head Peak (11,400ft). Finally the fantastically eroded Bryce Canyon with its Queen's Parlour trail before the Grand Canyon adventure. A better variety of walks would be hard to find.

Yosemite Trails

In the middle of all this we spent a few days in the Yosemite Valley, one of the wonders of the natural world. The view from Glacier Point, 3214ft above

the valley floor, is truly breathtaking as it sweeps down the canyon, taking in the various waterfalls and the unique Half Dome (8842ft) which, true to its name, is a huge dome of bare granite sliced off to present an awesome vertical face to the valley. From this vantage point the glacial origins of the valley are evident; a narrow V-shaped cleft with superb rock walls, the conquest of which, by various astonishing routes provided some of the most dramatic climbing of the post-war years. A walk known as the Four Mile Trail leads down to the valley floor from Glacier Point, zig-zagging lazily down on a delightful path, directly beneath the impressive Sentinel Rock (7038ft) which stands out like a granite spear. But the Four Mile Trail is a bit like the Three Musketeers - do you remember the secret of the Three Musketeers? There were *four* of them. The Four Mile Trail is nearly *five* miles long!

But the walk which remains uppermost in mind from Yosemite is the Mist Trail, which climbs up by the Vernal Falls to the Nevada Falls, following the Merced River. Both falls are very impressive - huge volumes of water pouring over high cliffs. As we entered the canyon of the Vernal Falls the noise was deafening. A narrow pathway, wet with spray, crawled past the falls and climbed by steep slippery steps up the side of the gorge. A fine mist covered everything until at last we broke free from the rocky confines of the gorge and emerged into hot Californian sunshine below the granite dome of Liberty Cap (7076ft). As we looked back, the sunlight and the mist combined to make a marvellous rainbow over the gorge.

It was another steep climb up to the rocky platform besides the Nevada Falls and awe-inspiring to watch and listen to the huge cataract. At 594ft it is almost twice the height of Vernal Falls but unlike Vernal, these falls were without grace or form; they were brutal, impressing by their sheer bulk and power.

We lay on the broad sun-soaked granite platform where the river tipped over the cliff edge, eating lunch and listening to the roar of the waters. Soon it was time to be off again, following the famous John Muir Trail back to the valley. We descended gradually through the woods, with superb views back to Liberty Cap and Half Dome, the peaks standing clearly etched against the blue Californian sky. We passed the entrance to the mysterious looking Illilouette Gorge and before long emerged on the main valley road. The frequent and free valley bus whisked us to Yosemite Village for a nice cooling ice-cream.

It is trails rather than tracks which excite most attention these days. A trail, or long-distance footpath, is a series of linked tracks traversing a particular area and often with some underlying theme. Frequently the link is the area

The easy 4-Mile Trail in Yosemite offers wonderful views of the valley

itself - the Tour of Mont Blanc, for example, or the Corsican High Level Route - but sometimes it is based on something else: the Way of St James, from Le Puy in France to Compostella in Spain, is an old pilgrim trail, or the Robert Louis Stevenson Trail in southern France, which follows the route taken by Stevenson in his famous *Travels with a Donkey*. Trails are very numerous and diverse, found in many countries and of all sorts of length, from two or three days to several weeks. The Way of St James, for instance, is a thousand miles long whilst the Pacific Crest Trail, from the Mexican border to Canada, is 2598 miles - a formidable hike! Most trails are much shorter, often designed to last a week or two. (A list of some of the better known ones is given on p.52.)

Trails are usually waymarked to help the walker distinguish the right path to take, or even, on rocky ground, to show the way in the absence of any distinguishable track. In theory all you have to do is follow the correct mark all the way from start to finish, but it is seldom that simple. A painted double horizontal stripe - generally red and white - on a tree or boulder is the usual waymark, though there are variants - I have seen yellow triangles in Austria and Switzerland, sometimes numbered (you need to know what number of path you require before setting off!) and in Norway they use a letter T. The painted stripes can incorporate some simple instructions - if the stripe bends to the left or right that means the route bends the same way, so you need to look out for a junction in the path; if the stripes form a cross it means turn back, because you have gone the wrong way. There's a streak of wilful playfulness - or perhaps it is sadism - in the people who apply waymarks. The marks are seldom where you need one most and often plentiful where you don't need one at all.

In forests you should beware false waymarks - forestry workers have a practice of marking trees with painted stripes for their own purposes, and these can sometimes be very confusing. There was a notorious example of this on the popular GR5 near the French village of Abondance, which confused many walkers until the authorities got round to clearing things up.

In some upland areas cairns (piles of stones) are used to indicate a route but these should always be treated with a great deal of circumspection. False cairns are very common and are obviously misleading. In the higher mountains some mountaineers object to cairns, claiming that if you can't navigate without cairns, you shouldn't be there at all and that cairns detract from the mountain environment. Mmm. I have been up quite a few mountains in my time, and I tell you there have been times of mist and storm when I've been glad to come across a cairn!

Probably the most comprehensive system of waymarked footpaths in the world exists in France. These paths are known as Grandes Randonnées, or GR for short, and they generally have a number - the Corsican High Level Route is the GR20, for example, whilst the GR5 traverses the Alps from Lake Geneva to the Mediterranean. They are supervised by the Comité National des Sentiers de la Grande Randonnée of the Fédération Française de la Randonnée Pédestre: sentiers are footpaths, so these are footpaths for big walks ie. long-distance trails. They are supplemented by regional paths (GRP) and local paths (PR). There are dozens of routes covering the entire country in an intricate network. They are shown on the French IGN maps and IGN map 903 is a comprehensive map showing them all.

Other countries have similar networks though not so well developed and there are even cross-Europe routes known - what else? - as E-routes.

All these various routes have their waymarks and they offer simple accommodation in the form of bunkhouses or gîtes d'étape along the way. In mountain areas the accommodation may well be in the huts owned by the various Alpine clubs - though the word 'hut' is something of a misnomer; a hangover from the early days of alpinism when the mountain huts were literally just that. Apart from a few bivouac shelters of interest only to dedicated alpinists and in impossible situations, huts in the Alps are really simple mountain hotels offering dormitory accommodation and meals. Beyond the Alps the situation is different; huts can be very basic and they may be self-catering only. The most basic hut I have ever stayed at was the celebrated Camp 5 deep in the Mulu Hills of the Borneo jungle (see Ch 4) - a floor, a roof and four half-height walls. Alas! Progress dictates that this romantic shelter will soon be replaced.

Although many long distance trails can be back-packed, either camping or finding accommodation as and when you can, the advantage of using an adventure travel company is that you get prearranged accommodation, allowing you to walk with just a light day sack and camera. The rest of your gear is carried for you. This has a great deal of appeal, especially to older or less experienced walkers.

I've come across two methods of this. In the first method, exemplified by the firm called Alternative Travel, two highly qualified leaders accompany each group, one to act as a guide and the other to drive the Land Rover which accompanies the party. As the walkers struggle over the hills and dales, the Land Rover drives round (sometimes many miles) and meets them at some idyllic spot for lunch. Weary walkers arrive to find a sumptuous spread laid out for them with wine cooling in the stream! After lunch they continue to the hotel and dinner. Most days are not too long, and the Land Rover is always there at lunch time should anyone feel incapable of the second half, so this is walking at its most sybaritic. Naturally enough, it does not come cheap and most clients are professional people, often doctors.

With this method all you need do is follow the leader, so there is no responsibility - but perhaps there's no challenge either, and some people may want the challenge. The system used by a company called Headwater does without the leaders. There is no back-up vehicle and you carry your own lunch! The company pre-books your accommodation, a regional representative conducts you from the nearest railway station to the start of the tour, and, provided with map and guide leaflet, you make your way from hotel to hotel. The hotel staff move your heavy baggage to the next hotel and so on, so you still only carry a light day sack. The system is said to have been devised in Germany and it works well.

Many adventure treks take place in Third World countries and, for the novice especially, a guided tour offers distinct advantages over trying to go it alone. Travelling alone I have spent days waiting for a trekking permit and on one memorable trip to Africa no fewer that five planes failed to turn up, even though the trip was organised, if that is the word, by the government concerned. With an experienced tour company these things don't seem to happen; for one thing, the British company itself will not be doing the organising at ground level - there'll be a local agent, who knows just what is wanted and how to get it. In addition, before setting out there will be lots of information and advice on inoculations, visas, money changing and kit - though not all of this may be up to scratch and you would be well advised to heed the advice given in this book!

The brochure will explain whether a tour is a backpacking trip or whether porters will be employed. If the former you may end up carrying all your gear plus food and tents, though it is more usual for some porterage to be employed, if only for the tents and cooking. On the Grand Canyon crossing, for example (see Ch 7), our guide carried the cooker but we all carried food and in the Canyon (like all American national parks) all trash has to be carried out - there's no burning, no burying. It was so warm that tents were not needed; we bivouacked beneath a deep purple sky littered with a million diamond-bright stars.

Etruscan Trails

I stood on the crest of a steep, densely wooded slope, shielding my eyes from the strong Italian sunlight. Below my feet the woods tumbled down to a broad, deep gorge and across, on the other side of the chasm, was one of the most remarkable sights in Europe - the little town of Pitigliano, incredibly perched high on a tufa crag, inviolate and seemingly inaccessible.

Pitigliano was one of the great cities of Etruria, that mysterious state founded by the Etruscans who, for several centuries before the birth of Christ, existed in central Italy. Nobody knows where they came from and ultimately they were destroyed and absorbed by the rising power of Rome, but they left behind them an astonishing range of art: jewellery and golden ornaments, ceramics of great beauty and painted tombs. There were statues too and what little remains of their architecture indicates that this also was highly

Crossing the River Stellata in Tuscany.
Deeper streams call for more precautions

sophisticated. It was an entire civilization about which we know practically nothing because nobody has succeeded in fully deciphering the language.

The Etruscans established cities like Pitigliano, Orvieto and Sovana (to give them their modern names) which traded with one another along properly constructed roads, many of which have long been forgotten, hidden by the undergrowth of centuries. The aim of our little group was to find and follow as many of these ancient tracks as possible and it turned out to be a remarkable voyage of discovery. Christopher Whinney, the head man at Alternative Travel had done the original research, spending several weeks exploring the countryside north of Rome, between Montemerano and Orvieto, finding tracks lost for centuries.

We spent the first day sampling the hot, sulphurous waters of the River Stellata at Molina del Bagno, clinging on to the tufa rocks to save being swept away by the current. I've never been keen on thermal baths but it seems my luck to come across them everywhere - Iceland, the Azores, New Zealand, the USA and even Uzbekistan! The smell is like rotten eggs - the sulphuretted hydrogen we all loved to make in the chemistry lab at school - though why rotten eggs should be regarded as a cure for rheumatics I can't imagine. The river tipped over a cascade every ledge of which was draped with bathers, like guillemots on nesting sites at some remote sea cliff. I fully expected someone to dive off and pick up a fish - though any fish in the Stellata would be ready parboiled. The temperature was 37°C (98°F). We came away refreshed if slightly malodorous.

The countryside across which we walked during the next few days consisted of rolling hills and deep gorges, our footsteps either on *strada bianca*, very similar to our bridleways at home, or on narrow tracks through fields and woods - apart from the Etruscan roads themselves, that is. Some of the tracks were steep and rugged, with an occasional shallow river crossing, but at least in the woods there was some relief from the unseasonably hot weather; it seemed that late June had arrived in early May. Many of the paths were obviously little used and frequently we would burst out of thick jungle into some forgotten glade dominated by a tufa crag holding some long abandoned dwelling or chapel.

Towards the late afternoon of the second day we came to the gorge of the River Meleta with the astonishing view of Pitigliano. David, our leader, plunged into the thicket like a bear after honey and we followed, only to discover it was as steep as he'd promised. There was no path but after some vertical thrashing through the undergrowth we landed on a narrow track in the depths of the woods. This ran parallel with the valley and was obviously man-made and very old. We followed it through a strange cutting until, bathed in the mysterious green light of the forest, rock carvings appeared; the decayed entrances to ancient tombs. They were the first Etruscan tombs we'd seen and they reminded me forcibly of the rock tombs at Petra in Jordan. Nor was this the only similarity because as we worked our way down to the foot of the gorge we found ourselves following great slots cut in the rock, just like the *siq* at the entrance to Petra, but smaller. Some historians believe the Etruscans came from the Middle East, but it is easy to get carried away by fanciful theories - in this case the Etruscans came several centuries before the Nabateans who built Petra!

Still, the great rock cuttings are a mystery. Why not build zig-zags as modern road builders do to overcome steep slopes? The only feasible explanation, it seemed to me, was that the rock cut out was used for building the town. Originally wide enough for a narrow cart, the cuttings are now choked with debris, but their discovery by Chris Whinney was a great find.

In the museum at Pitigliano we saw our first Etruscan pottery and wondered at its beauty. No wonder the great English potter Josiah Wedgwood, centuries later, called his own pottery works Etruria.

Next day we walked to another ancient site, Sovana, where there are more tombs and some fine medieval churches. The walking was mostly on *strada bianca* but it also involved the crossing of a deep gorge where we were startled to see several snakes slide away into the dense undergrowth. Snakes are not the first thing that comes to mind when you are thinking of walking in Italy! Beyond the gorge, fields and hedgerows were ablaze with spring flowers including asphodel, borage, wild gladioli and, everywhere, poppies in profusion.

We watched a wedding in the 12th-century church of Santa Maria in the little square at Sovana. The square was chock-a-block with Ferarris and Mercedes, because this was a union between two powerful banking families from Rome - apparently the tiny church is very much the 'in' place to be married, despite the huge cathedral just a couple of hundred yards up the road. In fact, there's more to Sovana than meets the eye; the meal laid on in the evening by the *Albergo Etrusca* was truly outstanding: nettle soup, wild asparagus with pasta, sausage with roast potato, kid with green salad, fresh fruit salad and a fine selection of wines. No wonder Alternative Travel are famed for their meals.

After Sovana the going got tougher. Little used paths through dense woods alternated with abandoned Etruscan roads, some of which had probably never been walked for centuries. We passed below the hilltop village of Sorano where many fine houses have been abandoned because the cliff on which they stand is crumbling away. Efforts are being made to shore up the crag, but the roofless, eyeless buildings seemed destined to tumble into the gorge below. The village of Vitozza was also abandoned, and had been for 300 years, but the ruins are preserved and identified for the curious minded traveller. Here too we discovered a magnificent Etruscan tomb perched on the edge of a cliff and half hidden by undergrowth. For how many centuries did the ghost of some noble Etruscan look out from his tomb over that magnificent valley?

Our walk then took us through more open countryside to the large volcanic lake of Bolsena, where we stayed at the town of the same name; a place of steep alleyways crowned by an ancient and forbidding castle. When the Roman legions crushed the last of the Etruscans at Orvieto and destroyed the town they transferred the survivors to this place. It is famed today for its light white wine known as *Est! Est!! Est!!!*, so named because in the old days a bishop travelling across Tuscany sent his servant on ahead to try out the hostelries where his master could stay. If the wine was good he was to write Est! on the gate. On his arrival at Bolsena he was so overcome by the quality (or quantity!) of the local wine he wrote Est! Est!! Est!!!

In the middle of the lake is a large private island called Bizantia which we were privileged to visit. It has been called the most beautiful island in the world - a pardonable exaggeration, easily forgiven when you've seen the place. It is a little idyll, with its palazzo and ruined chapels at present being restored by an Italian nobleman, who has an eye for beauty.

From Bolsena we walked by fields and woods to the crest of a ridge overlooking Orvieto, piled majestically tower on tower, like a city from Hans Anderson, or perhaps Walt Disney. Much larger that Pitigliano, Orvieto has the same medieval atmosphere, but there's more to explore - the great striped cathedral with its magnificent artwork, the encircling walls with a plethora of other churches, all incredibly ancient, and the unique Pozzo di San Patricio, which is a remarkable well dug in the 16th century, 62m deep and 13.4m wide, with a double helix stairway cleverly incorporated in its walls.

And of course, the famous Orvieto Classico wine. Tell you what, if the bishop's servant had tried this wine he'd have added another Est!

There are few places in the world as scenically attractive as the South Island of New Zealand. There are mountains, moors, swift flowing rivers, forests and sandy beaches. Unfortunately there's also a good deal of rain and the pesky sandflies, but you can't have everything and at least it is free from snakes, scorpions, bears and the tummy bugs which make some other areas less attractive. Walking is well catered for - there are plenty of huts, some fairly primitive, and numerous developed trails both for single day and multi-day walks. It is the latter which are most famous - the 55km Hollyford Track, the 77km Heaphy Track and about a dozen others, of which the best known is the world-renowned Milford Track in the Fiordland National Park: 54km through the rainforest from Lake Te Anau over the MacKinnon Pass to the Milford Sound on the west coast.

With the exception of the Copland Track, near Mt Cook, which requires some alpine experience, most New Zealand tracks are straightforward, sometimes strenuous, but often quite easy. Some, however, do require river crossings and if the water is high or the stream swift flowing this can be a danger. The force of water is often underestimated - if it comes up to the knees and is swiftly flowing you stand a good chance of being swept off your feet, though with gentler flows it is possible to go chest deep (as in the River Narrows, Ch 7, and the Headhunters' Trail Ch 4). Always choose the widest, and therefore shallowest, place to cross.

In a guided party the guide should be carrying a rope to help the party across a river. This technique needs some mastering and is best left to experts to implement. Without a rope there are two methods available. In the first (and best) three people form a triangle with arms firmly linked, heads close together and legs apart. One man faces upstream, so the other two are side on to the flow. They move across crabwise, only one moving at a time. In the second method the group forms a single file facing upstream, hands on the shoulders of the one in front and supporting him. All move across sideways, taking small steps. It helps if the front man has a stout stick or a trekking pole.

Crossing singly is a nervy business requiring good judgement and should be avoided if there is an alternative (some of the New Zealand tracks, for instance, have high level alternatives which are longer but safer). Choose the widest and shallowest part, face the flow, keep legs apart and use a trekking pole as a third leg. Try to angle the crossing diagonally into the flow.

In some places streams are crossed by rope or wire bridges, often with just a single strand for the feet. I have always found the firmest footing to be where the footrope is tied to the sideropes - you can step from knot to knot. On wire place the feet across the wire in Chaplinesque fashion and step gingerly!

A Walk by the Sea - The Abel Tasman Coast Track, New Zealand

One of the easiest and most unusual of New Zealand's classic walks is a three day hike along the northern shore of South Island, where the Abel Tasman National Park fringes Tasman Bay. It is a popular walk through stunning coastal scenery beginning at Marahau and finishing at Totaranui, where a ferry can be caught to go back to the start. It can be continued round Separation Point to Wainui and a return made by bus, but this takes another day and is not as popular as the three day hike. Even less popular is to return by the inland track which takes a further three to five days. The Department of Conservation (DOC) has four huts on the coastal path which provide bunks, heating and water but no cooking facilities. A DOC permit is required. There are camping facilities too, and another four huts provide accommodation on the inland trail.

However, as on some other New Zealand trails (the Milford and Routeburn, for instance) there is a parallel series of private huts; in this case operated by the Abel Tasman National Park Enterprises, a private company which operates guided tours along the walk and also own the launches for the ferry service. This is a unique variation on the guided walk theme for though you only need carry a day sack as usual, the rest of your gear is taken from hut to hut by boat!

I drove up from Kaikoura on the east coast, where I'd spent a day whale watching, through the vineyards of Blenheim and the little town of Nelson to Marahau Lodge at the entrance to the National Park. Next day I set out with a small group - Americans and Swiss - across the boardwalk of the Marahau inlet to pick up the coast path on its first leg to Tinline Bay. The walking was easy, the path well made and the views of the well wooded coastline stunning. We had lunch at Stilwell Bay then climbed a small saddle to cross to Torrent Bay, a wide mouthed inlet. The tide was out and this enabled us to save 40 minutes by walking across the estuary, though the mud was unpleasant. There was still the Torrent River to cross as it made its way through the mudflats, but it wasn't deep and before long we all arrived at Torrent Bay Lodge, a simple but comfortable homestead.

We carried our boots across the bay to save them from the mud, but I have never been a barefoot enthusiast, unlike our guide, David, who did the whole trip barefoot from start to finish. As the paths were liberally sprinkled with all sorts of pine needles and prickly leaves I asked him how he managed to escape without lacerating his feet and he reckoned that experience had taught him to sense whether anything he was treading on was going to hurt and adjusted his step accordingly. This strikes me as a high risk strategy, but I pass it on to anyone interested in acquiring the technique! Nevertheless, boots are a nuisance on this walk (I think it is the only walk I know where this is the case) and the ideal walking footwear would be old trainers that you can wade in, beach stroll in and use on the paths. On this walk, without any doubt, your feet are going to get wet, you'll get mud up your legs and sand in your toes.

Next day it was drizzling as we faced the steep climb out of Torrent Bay. There was more up and down work today and greater variety of scenery too. We climbed the Saddle and dropped down to the Falls River which we crossed on a swingbridge. The river looked like a jungle stream all hung about with tree ferns and tall rimu trees. Then came another ridge crossing to Bark Bay where there is a DOC hut in which we had our lunch and watched the rain drift away.

It was another climb out of Bark Bay - this time 120m - before dropping down to Tonga Quarry, where once granite had been hewn. Several abandoned blocks lay on the shore. It can never have been a large quarry, but it must have been one of the most beautifully sited; golden sands, exotic trees and the bluest of blue seas. Across the water lay Tonga Island, which is the centre of a marine reserve stretching from Bark Bay to the next large inlet at Awaroa. It has a large seal colony and all plant and animal life is totally protected.

Another hundred metre climb above the cliffs and then we dropped down to the idyllic beach of Onetahuti, a kilometre of golden sand stretching in an arc below the forest fringe. The walk at this point follows the shore and at the northern end there was a bit of a hiatus whilst we waited for the tide to recede. Wading may be fun but it can be very deep just here. Time to sit and stare whilst the waters crept back.

From the beach came the biggest climb of the day - 120m - over the Tonga Saddle to the largest and most complex of the Abel Tasman bays, Awaroa. With the tide out we were able to wade across to the Awaroa Lodge where I had a beer with Terry Knight who has set up the lodge and cafe as a centre for exploring the Park. Since it can be reached by boat, this is an alternative way of seeing Abel Tasman National Park for those who don't want to follow the trail.

It was only a short step to our own accommodation for the night, the Homestead Lodge. The Homestead at Awaroa looks like a large Victorian villa and in fact such a villa, called Meadowbank, was built on the site in 1884 but gradually fell into disuse and was completely rebuilt with extensions to make the Homestead Lodge in 1994. It is so called because it was the original family home of the Wilsons who own the company running the tours. The food and

The Registan Square in Samarkand, Uzbekistan, is one of the great monuments of the
Islamic world. This doorway is to the Tilla Kar madrasseh in the square (Ch 3)

A vaulted bazaar in Bukhara, Uzbekistan, with the Tower of Death in the background from which victims were flung (Ch 3)
The Kay-Darvaz Gate at Khiva, Uzbekistan, with the stump of the Kalta Minar behind. Never completed, the minar was intended to be the highest tower of its kind in Central Asia. Khiva is lovingly restored (Ch 3)

The ruins of the Shariah Ark at ancient Merv, the very heart of Central Asia (Ch 3)

A desert yurt near the River Oxus (Ch 3)

Ancient cities abound in Central Asia. Here a team of Italian archeologists are excavating Nisac, in Turkmenistan, once the capital of the mighty Parthians (Ch 3)

The Long Trail in Vermont travels through the forest all the way to the Canadian border (Ch 4)

The Camel's Hump, Vermont. In the fall the forest becomes a carpet in shades of red and gold (Ch 4)

The Kiutagongas Falls in the Oulanka National Park, Finland. The Bears' Ring is a long distance walk through the forest near here (Ch 4)

An evening walk near Leopard's Rock in the bush country of Kruger National Park, South Africa. Walking is strictly controlled - only a few parties each year - and for safety reasons each is accompanied by armed rangers (Ch 4)

Approaching the Chalet Lookout near Fox Glacier, New Zealand. The West Coast of South Island has miles of impenetrable forest - and vicious sandflies! (Ch 4)

A limestone cave forms the cookhouse at the celebrated Camp 5 in Mulu National Park, Sarawak (Ch 4)

Wading a jungle river on the Headhunters' Trail, Sarawak (Ch 4)

accommodation are superb.

During the night there was a violent rainstorm and it was still raining heavily as we set out next day. There is a problem at Awaroa - you can only cross the inlet some two hours before and after low tide - a daunting undertaking anyway because the other shore seems such a long way off. There is no way round through the impenetrable bush. On the morning of our departure the tide was high, but since we were on a guided tour a boat was provided by the Homestead to take us across the water, the whirring of its outboard motor reverberating off the forest all round.

We landed on the far beach, picked up the trail and crossing another saddle fetched up about mid-day at Totaranui, the end of the walk. The rain had stopped so we ate lunch on the beach waiting for the ferry boat which turned out to be a surprisingly big one. The water was deep enough at Totaranui for it to come right in and drop a gangplank. Passengers disembarked and we scrambled aboard and with a dull throb of powerful engines the boat turned about and sped off down the coast. I was disembarking at Awaroa to have lunch with Terry Knight, but here the water was too shallow for the big boat, so passengers were transferred to and from the shore by a smaller craft and I found myself jumping from boat to boat in a heavy swell and finally wading ashore, like John Wayne invading Iwojima, since even the little boat couldn't quite make it. I had lunch with very wet feet!

2
Peaks and Precipices

Long-distance walks like the ones I have described in Tuscany and the Abel Tasman National Park are not difficult and can be very enjoyable. There are dozens more like them. Sometimes, however, the walks are a bit tougher - mountains are involved.

It may be that this simply means extra physical demands will be made - steeper slopes, rougher tracks, worse weather - but there may be other factors too such as altitude sickness or exposed scrambling. The average person can cope with all these - *provided he is prepared.* They are not the preserve of the dedicated mountaineer and indeed mountain treks are the most popular of all. Some of the problems can be illustrated by two of the world's most popular walks.

Walking Round Mont Blanc

When it comes to long-distance footpaths, the Tour du Mont Blanc must be very near the top of the pops. Tourists of the hardier sort have been following its course for at least two centuries. The theme of the walk is, of course, to circumnavigate the highest mountain in Western Europe together with its satellites. The northern part of the walk is in France, the southern part in Italy, and there's a little bit of Switzerland thrown in for good measure. Seven delectable valleys penetrate into the heart of the massif and the TMB, as it is usually called, visits each in turn. The ridges which separate the valleys are crossed by high passes and this is what makes it more serious than the average French GR. Funnily enough, a wilderness experience it ain't - the popularity of the route ensures that there are always people around.

Pat Hurley and I had chosen the beginning of July in which to do the walk, before the start of the French school holidays. We figured this would give us a better chance of finding accommodation, for we had booked nothing in advance and didn't fancy camping. It is always a risk, chancing on accommodation like this, but nowadays several firms have the TMB in their brochure so the worry about accommodation and the humping of a big pack can be overcome.

We began our journey by catching a train! The track belongs to the Tramway du Mont Blanc, an electric cog-wheel railway that makes an incredible journey up the long spur of mountain called Le Prarion, heading towards Mont Blanc. The Toytown cars, dwarfed by their immense environment, begin their journey at Le Fayet, crawl through the streets there then haul themselves up through St Gervais to the Col de Voza and beyond, ending high up in the stony wastes of Pierre Ronde below the Aiguille du Goûter. It is a remarkable tram ride by any standard.

We got off at the Col du Voza and strolled down from the ridge through the Val Montjoie to the little village of Les Contamines. It had rained, on and off, throughout the day, but as we reached Contamines the sun broke through and lit up the fields full of the most incredible array of alpine flowers one could imagine. En route we had discovered that the official TMB has variants here and there - and that a TMB variant is *always* harder than the original! In fact, this is a good rule of thumb for most long distance walks: *the variants are always harder*.

Next day, in improving weather, we continued up the valley past the ancient chapel of Notre Dame de la Gorge, its white walls and baroque splendour contrasting sharply with the dark forest round about. From the chapel an old Roman road climbed up steeply - this is one of the principal ways the Romans invaded Gaul - until it entered an upland vale which took us past the Nant Borrant mountain inn to the little restaurant at La Balme. There were views back down the Val Montjoie and to the great peaks of the Miage. As we sat on the terrace enjoying a coffee we could see that the way ahead, climbing towards the Col du Bonhomme, looked steep and what was more disconcerting, flecked with snow patches. We realised that this probably meant that the top of the pass was snow-covered and so it proved. In fact we met the snow well before the top.

There shouldn't have been snow - it was July, after all - but it just goes to show the unpredictability of mountain treks. In most years the way to the Col du Bonhomme would just be a steep stony track, but the previous winter had been a hard one, with lots of snowfall and the uncertain spring had failed to bring the thaw. So the snow still lay deep, gleaming with half hidden ice patches.

The passage of other walkers was marked by a steep, slippery, slushy runnel, which we eschewed. Instead we kicked our own steps in the time honoured manner of mountaineers - kick with the boot toe slightly downwards, press a little to compact things, then step up on it. This leaves a perfectly shaped hole in which the next person can step. Every so often we alternated leads and it was very satisfactory to look back as we neared the top to see that neither of us had broken the steps; there was a perfect ladder for the next trekker who might pass this way!

We reached the Col du Bonhomme (2329m) and looked down into the barren wilds of Beaufortain but that was not our way. From the Col du Bonhomme the TMB goes to the Col de la Croix du Bonhomme by swinging round a steep cirque below the rocky tower of the Roche du Bonhomme.

Normally this would not present a problem but Pat and I gazed with some concern at the sheer white slopes of snow which now covered the cirque. Still, there was nothing for it but to try. Tentatively we edged along the groove that had been beaten in the snow by countless feet. How I wished I'd had an ice-axe! It wasn't to be the last time on this trip either! Here and there the groove had collapsed where some poor devil had broken the snow and slid down a foot or two - that must have been heart-stopping for them!

However, we were both accustomed to crossing snow slopes, though usually with axe and crampons, so our insecurity was short lived and before long we breasted the Col (2476m) and could see below us the Refuge de la Croix du Bonhomme; a reconstruction of the original hut destroyed during the war. Beyond the hut low mountains rolled away only to rise again into a perfect snow cone in the distance, Mont Pourri (3781m). The refuge was a happy hut; not filled to overflowing but with lots of good companionship. Most people there were doing the TMB.

It was a steep descent the following day into the Vallée des Glaciers, a long narrow valley which led us up a tiresome metalled road to a little refuge called Les Mottets. At the head of the valley rose the Aiguilles des Glaciers, with their long sweeping skirt of ice, the Glacier des Glaciers - a name which is definitely OTT! On the left was the rocky peak of Mont Tondu whilst on the right we could see our path climbing steeply up a rough pasture towards another col, the Col de la Seigne (2516m), which marks the frontier between France and Italy.

The climb to the col was not particularly long or arduous, although at the top we met the snow again. From here, though, we got our first view of the magnificent southern flanks of Mont Blanc. The old monarch is just a great mound of snow when seen from the Chamonix valley, noble in size, though with few features of distinction, but on this Italian flank it throws down great jagged ridges of savage majesty, unparalleled throughout the Alps. The spectacular Aiguille Noire de Peuterey by itself would be enough to make you draw in breath, pointing like a huge black arrowhead to the sky, but there is also the lovely ice-draped Aiguille de Tré la Tête, rising from the Lex Blanche glacier. The Lex Blanche itself lay directly below us, a desolate cirque which forms the head of the long Val Veni. Down we plunged through the snow, past the extraordinary Pyramides Calcaires, to climb up again to the splendid Rifugio Elisabetta where we spent the night.

Next day we made our way to Courmayeur, which despite the building of the Mont Blanc tunnel and all the ensuing traffic, has retained a lot of its old-world charm. To reach it, however, meant following a road down the valley which is very popular with touring motorists, most of whom seem to be in a hurry. Fortunately one of the TMB's many diversions comes to the rescue - a steep track climbs out of the valley onto a shoulder of Mont Favre, at a height of 2375m. From here there is a tremendous view across the valley; a wonderful panorama encompassing the whole south side of the Mont Blanc range. We got the map out and identified the various peaks. From this high vantage point too, Mont Blanc itself is seen in proper perspective for the first time. How it dominates with its great height and what imperial majesty is shown in its huge buttresses of rock and ice!

Although our climb gave us great views of the mountains it also brought us back to the snowline. The little Lac Chécrouit, in which the Mont Blanc range is usually reflected, had vanished under snow and all round were steep - very steep - slopes. A slip here would not have been pleasant and once again I longed for my trusty ice-axe. With an axe you have a prop to rest against the slope which aids balance, but more important, if you slip you can use the axe as a brake. I used to demonstrate this during winter courses at an outdoor centre in the Lakes; beginning first with a gentle slide and how to stop it, then a slide starting on your back so you have to roll over and stop it and finally a slide in which the victim shoots down on his back head first. They say practice makes perfect and fortunately, like abseiling, once you've done it you actually enjoy repeating it.

We spent the next couple of days in Courmayeur before moving on. The weather had turned bad on us and even as we climbed out of the Val Ferret towards the Grand Col Ferret and the Swiss border it was mizzle and drizzle. Strangely, although this col is the highest on the official TMB at 2537m (some variants are higher) there was no snow lying. It was a steady plod to the top and a rather pleasant descent past the cowsheds at Le Peule and through the woods to meet the valley floor at Les Ars-dessous. As we reached the pretty little hamlet of Ferret the rain stopped and we strolled on to the larger village of La Fouly where we spent the night. It is confusing that on both sides of the watershed the valley should be called Ferret, but they are usually distinguished by nationality - the Swiss Val Ferret, the Italian Val Ferret.

We had good mountain gear so we came to no harm in the mist and rain, but bad weather such as that can lead to exposure, a condition which needs to be taken seriously from the outset. Hard physical exertion combined with bad weather can cause a severe chilling of the body so that core temperature is lost and this shows itself in unreasonableness, tiredness, cold, lethargy and in worse cases slurred speech, blurred vision, violent shivering and ultimately collapse. Severe cases can lead to death. The medical term is hypothermia and the treatment is to protect the victim immediately from further effort, to wrap them up warmly (a sleeping bag is great for this) and give them hot sweet drinks. But not alcohol - the romantic vision of a St Bernard suddenly appearing with a cask of brandy round its neck is unlikely to happen and if it does, just remember it's bad for you! A victim of hypothermia should be examined by a doctor as soon as possible.

Wind chill is the greatest factor in exposure. Air temperature is lowered even by the slightest breeze and the stronger the wind the lower it gets. One of the main aims if exposure is suspected is to get out of the wind. It may sound strange, but even on a glacier it is safer to crawl into a shallow crevasse, an icy tomb, than to stay on the surface in the wind.

The Swiss Val Ferret is one of the most idyllic in the Alps, with cuckoo-clock chalets whose window boxes are a blaze of geraniums, set on rocky knolls amidst dark copses of larch and spruce. We wandered down it next day in bright sunshine, until at the village of Issert we began the steep climb up to Champex. Just before the village is reached there is the Darbellay stream to cross, but fortunately for us the water wasn't high and we were able to cross with relative ease. Champex, set on a shoulder of hill by a charming lake, was once a favoured resort of the wealthy during *la belle époque*, but now relies mainly on day trippers from the Rhône valley. We stayed the night, then walked over the Bovine Alp to the motel at La Forclaz. This was a lovely walk with wide views over the Rhône and across to the Oberland.

Next day we left Switzerland and returned to France. From La Forclaz the TMB descends into the valley of Trient before climbing again to the Col du Balme, but we could see no virtue in losing a thousand feet of height and so we elected to follow a variant which contoured round the mountainside, avoiding the height loss. Our way led along a good path by the side of a *bisse* or water course - what we would call a leat, in England - which took us to the snout of the Trient Glacier; a tumble of blue ice. We crossed the issuing stream by a little bridge to a deserted hamlet called les Grandes where an amazing rock staircase climbed across a huge cliff face. Presumably the staircase had been built to reach the upper alpage at one time with sheep or cattle, but no effort had been spared to make it superior. It even had good iron hand-rails!

Once beyond the staircase we found ourselves on a steep mountainside with a view straight down to Trient which looked like a Legoland model, far below. It was disconcerting to find ourselves faced with several large snowfields. Nobody had preceded us on these slopes and the snow was hard, exhibiting a touch of iciness which raised our adrenalin considerably. Going across the snow meant kicking steps with the side of the boot and keeping in balance. Sometimes the steps came easily; sometimes it took several kicks to form even the smallest footledge. Once again the ice-axe would have been a boon. Had either of us slipped we would have shot down out of control for at least a hundred metres.

But we survived the experience and reached the Col du Balme, where a refuge-cum-restaurant marks the French frontier, and where the TMB re-enters the Chamonix valley. The view along the valley and across to the Aiguilles Rouges is superb, but better still is the breathtaking vista of Mont Blanc, floating high like a great white cloud with the spiky Aiguille Verte in the forefront.

A good track led down steeply to the hamlet of Le Tour, the highest village and end of the valley road. From here to Les Houches in the south the valley of the Arve is crowded with villages and hamlets, every one famous in mountaineering history. They are very popular with visitors, but the TMB avoids the valley altogether. Pat and I climbed up to the ridge of the Aiguilles Rouges, on the opposite side of the valley, the final leg of the walk. We traversed it for two days - an immensely satisfying rocky promenade along good paths and taking in the summit of le Brévent (2526m). All the way along there are superb and ever changing views across the valley to the Mont Blanc massif, which we had just circumnavigated.

Down eventually to Les Houches, where the roar of traffic was almost deafening after the solitude of the past few days. The Tour du Mont Blanc had more than lived up to its reputation - it undoubtedly is one of world's great walks.

From our experiences on the Mont Blanc walk you can see that weather is much more important on mountain walks than at lower levels. Bad weather clothing is a must and though you are likely to carry the basics in any case, it is a good idea always to have a spare sweater and gloves even in summer. And even if you prefer to walk in shorts, a pair of lightweight trousers should be carried in the day sack. The weather can change with amazing rapidity in the mountains.

Many people going on a mountain trek for the first time fear that frostbite is a major hazard - it is something they have heard of, and perhaps seen on adventure films. It can be a serious problem for mountaineers, but I have never seen real frostbite on an adventure trek. Extremely cold fingers are the worst you are likely to suffer, and only if you have inadequate gloves: the cure is to shove your hands down your crutch to restore warmth. The pain is excruciating as the blood surges back to the capillaries! Incidentally, gloves can be supplemented by wearing socks on top of them for extra warmth.

In some ways the sun is a much more potent enemy. You need to guard against heat stroke just as you must against exposure. Though I've been to some very hot countries the only time I have ever had heat stroke was in the Yorkshire Dales! It isn't pleasant - sickness and diarrhoea often result. Clothes need adapting to the situation - and drink plenty of water, preferably laced with some electrolyte such as Isostar to put back any minerals lost through sweating.

A high factor sun cream - factor 20 minimum if possible - is even more essential in the mountains than elsewhere because of the intensity of UV rays, and a lip salve is useful too. I use a good sun hat of the broad brimmed Norfolk type to protect my head, though I must confess that when I went on serious climbs in the Alps, in earlier days, I preferred to go hatless, or wore a protective helmet if the climb warranted it. A hat is too much of a nuisance when you are climbing.

The sun is certainly an important consideration when crossing glaciers as some mountain treks do. The UV rays can bounce back off the ice and cause severe burning so high factor block is more essential than ever. Bare flesh should be kept to a minimum - trousers not shorts, sleeves turned down and gloves. Lips suffer particularly badly so a good application of a lip salve is needed. This protection is needed even if the day is misty - the UV cuts through the mist and burns you just the same.

Continuous snow or ice also demands sun glasses to protect the eyes, or the result can be snow-blindness, which though not a permanent affliction is extremely painful.

Wearing gloves has a secondary use. A lot of the glaciers encountered on treks are dry glaciers - that is to say, they are of ice with no snow covering. This is good because you can see the crevasses and avoid them, but the ice is often very sharp and to fall on it can result in lacerated hands. A colleague of mine once went on the Arolla glacier in Switzerland and because it was a misty day didn't bother with sunblock and didn't wear gloves. He slipped and scraped his hands and his face ended up like a beetroot with lips that were cracked and blistered. *He was on the glacier for about an hour.*

Hut to hut tours in the Stubai mountains of Austria, or climbing some Norwegian peaks like Fannaraken or Galdhopiggen, are among the trips which involve simple glacier crossings. There will almost certainly be a beaten track and the risk of hidden crevasses or avalanches will be minimal.

One thing you are most unlikely to suffer from on a European mountain trek is altitude sickness. There may be some steep climbs and you may run out of puff from time to time, but the debilitating sickness and headaches only come at much higher altitudes. Having said that, there's a lot not known about the effect of altitude on the human body and cases have been recorded lower than 3700m - but rarely. 4500m is the height most start to feel the effects, if at all - I am one of those fortunate people seemingly unaffected, at least to about 6000m. I've never been higher and am unlikely to do so!

The Roof of the World - Trekking to Everest

Some say that the Circuit of Annapurna has replaced the Everest trek as the most popular of the famous Himalayan walks and one can see the attraction of a circular route rather than the in and back which is necessary for Everest. Some variety can be introduced, but only by making the trek much more serious.

This walk goes very high, usually to the summit of a hill called Kala Pattar which is 5625m or 18,450ft. It is necessary, therefore, to take time out to acclimatize on the way up and this is what the four of us - all friends from the Lancashire Mountaineering Club - decided to do. None of us had ever been to the Himalaya before, so we were grateful when we met up with friends from Sherpa, a travel company already making a name for themselves in trekking. They helped with visas and so forth in Kathmandu and we helped them test out a new bus, of all things - though what they were doing with a bus in Kathmandu escapes me now!

When John Hunt led his successful expedition of 1953 they walked all the way to Base Camp from Kathmandu, gradually increasing altitude and so acclimatizing gradually. However, this takes a long time and very few walk in all the way nowadays; it is usual to fly to the airstrip at Lukla, at the entrance to the Khumbu valley, and pick up porters there for the walk in. This in itself is an interesting experience for the airstrip is perched on the edge of a narrow valley and on landing or take-off the pilot has to be damned sure he knows what he's doing! At the time of our visit the airstrip edge was littered with wrecked planes, but Lukla has smartened up since then.

Because the weather wasn't at its best the regular flights to Lukla were not flying, so we hired a light plane piloted by a tough 'Nam veteran, who dodged in and out of the clouds, all the time listening to the weather reports on the radio. "The trouble with flying in Nepal, is sometimes the clouds have got rocks inside 'em," he said laconically. On the horizon we could see the Himalaya stretched out in a great white band: Everest, Kangchenjunga, Annapurna - or was it Dhaulagiri? No matter, they were all there, a magnificent tumbled mass.

The little plane landed with a defiant swoop onto the grass landing strip. In next to no time we had picked up our porters and were heading off up the valley. At Lukla the altitude is 2827m and by the evening we were actually lower, down to 2652m at Phakding, but in the succeeding days we made height in a series of big-dipper tracks - down, then up - but always a bit more up than down. At first the altitude is barely noticeable. The walking is in the deep gorge of the Dudh Kosi, whose name, 'Milk River', was aptly demonstrated. Boiling rapids, white with glacial dust from the foot of Everest, gave the river an angry appearance. The valley sides were aflame with the autumn tints of the berberis bushes.

We had decided to camp rather than use the Sherpa 'hotels', which in those days were hovels whose chief purpose was to serve the local beer called *chang*. Very good it is too, despite its milky colour and the bugs floating in it. We almost started a chang appreciation society, comparing brews as if they were Tetley and Theakstons. There is also a spirit known as *rakshi*, which is like a potent form of turpentine and, of course, the universal tea which the Sherpas brew in the kettle with milk and sugar included. It is the first thing that greets you in the morning - a brown arm pushed through the tent door and a cheery

"Chai, sahib!" Tea is a safer beverage than coffee on a trek because the water has to be boiled for tea but not for coffee, so there's less chance of tummy upsets. On one occasion as a guest in a Sherpa home we were offered black Tibetan tea which has rancid butter floating in it. It is disgusting and the problem is that if you drink it up quickly, eyes firmly shut, they simply refill it!

It was two days to the Sherpa 'capital' at Namche Bazar, approached at the end by a very steep pull of some 600m, and here we decided to camp for two nights, to allow us to acclimatize. Acclimatization is a funny business. If you rush up to great heights you are asking for trouble - slowly, slowly, catchee monkey - but if you hang about at great heights for too long you also begin to deteriorate. On our way up the valley we adopted the method of walking for two days and then staying put for a day before moving on. Strangely, it matters not if you go higher on a rest day - up a local hill for instance - provided you return to sleep at a lower level.

Altitude sickness is a wretched business altogether and has been known to mountain wanderers since the days when the Spaniards conquered Peru. The common symptoms are nausea, headache, loss of appetite and sleeplessness but some people are hardly affected at all and there seems no correlation with age, sex or level of fitness. Severe cases can lead to pulmonary oedema (water on the lungs) or cerebral oedema (water on the brain) which can cause death. Sadly, several trekkers die each year on the Everest trail. The only real cure - and it can be almost instantaneous - is to go down as quickly as possible. Unfortunately, anyone who is affected by mountain sickness will get it every time they go high. We took preventative diamox tablets, which were all the fashion at the time, but whether they worked or not is hard to say - certainly they didn't work for one companion who got no higher than Pheriche, 4253m.

One frightening effect of the altitude took place in our tent every night. The man I shared with had Cheyne-Stokes reaction, which is a loud and rapid breathing whilst asleep followed by a sudden stop. At first I feared the worst, but then the breathing started again and the whole thing was repeated. Apparently, it has no ill effects - but it scares the hell out of anyone listening!

Namche Bazar is a remarkable place, set in a bowl of the hills. A short way above it is Khumjung, a large village where Sir Edmund Hillary built his first schoolhouse. There is also a monastery where for a small charge the monks showed us a yeti scalp. It looked like a badly made red-haired wig, like something the old-fashioned clowns used to wear, and we couldn't bring ourselves to believe that one of the world's great mysteries had been reduced to this.

Above the village is the Everest View Hotel, which aims to provide four-star comfort for those who can't stand the rigours of the trail. Unfortunately this means flying in to the nearby airstrip and the sudden change in altitude

The Everest group seen from Kala Pattar, the usual end of the trek.
Everest is in the centre with its snow-covered west shoulder on the left
and the shapely Nuptse on the right

from the lowlands has led to serious altitude problems, even though oxygen is supplied to the bedrooms. We saw a very fat Japanese lady being carried down to the airstrip by a diminutive Sherpa in a rapid evacuation.

A steep track took us down to the river next day then climbed up to the monastery at Thyangboche. This is a real life Shangri La with views of some of the world's greatest - and most beautiful - mountains. Kangtega and Thamserku, the twin peaks of the Khumbu, glittered like ice coated sharks' fins against a blue sky but pride of place went to Ama Dablam, a lovely white spire of awesome beauty. In the distance we could see the Lhotse-Nuptse wall with the top of Everest just peeping over the crest.

Beyond Thyangboche the valley steadily became bleaker, first up to the huts at Pheriche where we again spent two nights, this time under the awesome obelisk of Taweche, soaring for 6500m overhead, then on to Lobuche and up the moraines of the Khumbu glacier to camp by a glacial lake, Gorak Shep. It was 5183m - roughly 17,000ft - and our highest camp. Above us soared the giant Pumori, 7146m, and its smaller rocky satellite Kala Pattar, 5625m.

The altitude was making us breathe very hard indeed as we struggled up the rocky slopes of Kala Pattar next day. It was sheer relief to reach the ridge line and follow it, briefly, to the summit. Here, at 18,500ft our eyes swept round the head of the Khumbu valley from Pumori to Changtse and Khumbutse and the superb ice-fluted buttresses of Nuptse, surely the most beautiful mountain in the world? Brooding over all was Everest itself, 8848m, and the highest mountain in the world: a great ugly brute of a mountain that over the years has seen some of the greatest feats of mountaineering.

We skittered down the scree from Kala Pattar and turned our backs on the high peaks. Four days later we were back in Kathmandu.

High mountain treks are probably the most popular kind of adventure travel. In the Peruvian Andes - the only area to rival the Himalaya - trips include the Inca Trail which leads to the fabulous ruins of Machu Picchu, the walk over the Punta Union pass in the Cordillera Blanca and the tour of the Cordillera Huayash, a tough walk which crosses eight high passes and is not for beginners. But the Himalaya and Karakorum are by far the most popular mountains for high treks, supplemented in recent years by adjacent areas which were previously off-limits - the mountains of Bhutan, Tibet, China and the Central Asian republics. Other doors have closed - Kashmir and Afghanistan are not available at present because of political unrest, and the Nanda Devi Sanctuary is often closed for environmental reasons. There's a wide variety of treks - some are gentle tours in Kulu, others are tough, like the Zanskar trek in Ladakh, the walk to Kanchenjunga base camp, or the ever popular walk up the Baltoro to Concordia below K2.

Surprisingly, perhaps, quite a number of the world's high mountains are accessible to the determined trekker who has no mountaineering qualifications. Elbruz in the Caucasus and Aconcagua are two popular destinations - the first being the highest mountain in Europe and the second the highest summit in the western hemisphere. Then there's Cotopaxi and various other volcanoes in Central and South America. They may not be technically difficult, but they all need determination and endurance. Such mountains as these should not be confused with what Nepal calls the 'trekking peaks', which are simply mountains not requiring an ascent fee, because they are relatively low by local standards but may well be proper climbs requiring some technical ability. Nevertheless, there are firms which will take you on these peaks and indeed there are firms which organise commercial ascents of the world's highest mountains, including Everest. I need hardly add that a certain degree of mountaineering experience is required before undertaking these!

The Roof of Africa

One of the most popular high mountains is Kilimanjaro (5896m), the highest mountain in Africa, which lies on the Kenya-Tanzania border. "As wide as all the world, great, high and unbelievably white in the sun" was how Hemingway described it in his famous story *The Snows of Kilimanjaro*. It certainly is wide, 50 miles by 30 miles and high too, one of the biggest volcanoes in the world, capped by snowfields and glaciers. There are three summits but only the central and highest, Kibo, attracts the walker because though the other two are fairly high one of them is a humpy moor of no attraction and the other - Mawenzi - a spiky crest of rock needles accessible only to the expert cragsman.

The whole area is a national park, with a centre at Merangu where a fairly stiff fee has to be paid to enter. Most walkers tackle the ordinary route which takes five days from the Park Gate, first through the forest to the Mandara Hut which is actually a series of Toblerone-shaped huts in an idyllic clearing. On the following day the forest is soon left behind. There is an abrupt transformation to rolling savannah with little rocky hillocks, which in turn gives way to landscape resembling an enormous rock-garden filled with heathers, helicrysums, giant lobelia and groundsel. Way below, the Masai Steppe stretches to the horizon with shimmering Lake Manyara in the far distance and huge volcanic cones, the highest of which is Meru, 4600m. The night is spent at the Horombo Hut, another collection of triangular shelters.

The altitude begins to bite at this stage. For some strange reason the effects seem to catch people sooner on this mountain than any other - perhaps it has something to do with the nearness of the Equator. The route is across a stony waste called the Saddle to the final hut, the Kibo, an old stone-built shelter at 4695m. Emergency oxygen is kept here. A lot of people find the altitude too much for them and abandon the ascent at this point.

The final cone rises above the hut like a gigantic slag heap. A start is made on the climb at 2 am, trudging up the scree like zombies in the dark, the pale glow from headlamps dancing off the rocks. As you near the top dawn breaks over Mawenzi peak and then you reach the rim of the caldera at Gillman's Point (5682m). More climbers give up here - it is another 213m and two hours to the actual summit, Uhuru Peak - but the determined ones press on to reach the roof of Africa.

Then it is swiftly down, zig-zagging easily across the slopes which were such a labour in the dark. After a drink at the Kibo Hut, it is back across the Saddle to spend the night at the Horombo Hut before leaving the park next day.

My own memories of Kilimanjaro are less than happy. From sheer carelessness I suffered bad sunburn on the way up and, ironically, was frustrated from reaching the top by a snowstorm!

S ome mountain ascents - and not necessarily high ones - are rocky and involve the use of hands as well as feet. This is known as scrambling and in Britain, at least, it has become a sport in its own right, something between walking and real rock climbing. On the Continent and in some other parts of the world, places that require scrambling are protected by fixed cables or chains, usually known simply as 'fixed ropes'. Such passages are often of short duration, but they are exposed and distinctly off-putting for anyone not used to heights.

I was once asked to try and cure a vicar of vertigo - perhaps he was afraid of not making the Final Ascent - and curiosity compelled me to undertake the task. He did not want to be a climber, but he did want to enjoy hillwalks and found that simple scrambles like Striding Edge in the Lake District terrified him. It was the first and only time I've come across real vertigo, but there is no doubt it *was* real. I took him to a local quarry where there were some small slabs and patiently got him to move up them a few feet, then across and down, then a bit further and so on. In the end he climbed a twenty foot slab (held on a rope, of course) and he paused to look down several times. Whether it finally cured him, I don't know.

Vertigo is just an extreme form of what many people fear when they first come across narrow, awkward ridges or ledges, overlooking a big drop. It is overcome by keeping calm and working out where you are going to place your hands and feet. If you keep your body away from the rock you can see more and balance better, and if you move just one hand or foot at a time you always have three points of contact with the rock.

Where there is a fixed rope, sometimes it is used as an aid, as in the ascent of Cone Rock in New Zealand (see Ch 4), but often it is just a reassurance on a narrow ledge. Such a one is found on the splendid little peak of Angels Landing (5990ft) in the Zion National Park, USA. This superb sandstone buttress seems impregnable when viewed from the canyon floor but a close inspection reveals a steep track which climbs into a hidden gulch known as Refrigerator Canyon, probably because it is shaded from the sun. A distinct col called Scout Lookout can be seen high above but once again the way seems impossible until an incredible solution is revealed - Walter's Wiggles, a path which zig-zags so sharply it is said you can see both ends of a horse at the same time! Built by the park supervisor, Walter Ruesch, back in 1919, it is an arduous ascent, especially in the hot sun.

From the Lookout a trail follows the ridge out towards Angels Landing, which at first you can't see because of an intervening hummock. The hummock proves something of a scramble and you become conscious that the ridge is narrowing. Fixed chains appear in exposed places. The final stretch of the ridge narrows further and leads with incredible exposure across a narrow col to the peak. At the col you can look straight down to the valley floor, 1500ft below. Fortunately there is plenty of room on top to recover from the ascent and look down on the wonderful Zion valley far below.

A Walk with the Gods: Via delle Bocchette, Brenta Dolomites

The ultimate in exposure is to be found amongst the limestone towers of the Eastern Alps, especially the Dolomites, where the nature of the rock has created long narrow ledges which can be protected by cables and joined to other ledges by metal ladders. In Italy such a route is called a *via ferrata*, in Austria a *klettersteig*. Sometimes they are quite short and form part of an ordinary Alta Via, as the various multi-day high level routes are known. At other times they are routes in themselves.

Some are very easy - like Striding Edge in Cumbria, say, or Crib Goch in Wales - but others are tricky and very, very exposed. They are protected by wire hawsers fixed to the rock wall. Sometimes there are 'stemples' or rungs to climb up or down from one ledge to another, sometimes short series of ladders and sometimes - here and there - ladders with over 300 rungs, bolted to a vertical wall! Hence the name, which means 'iron road'. The difference between the protection here and the odd fixed rope elsewhere is that here you are permanently attached.

You tie two longish slings round your waist, each with a karabiner. One sling is clipped to the hawser and runs along it as you travel. When you come to a bolt you clip the other sling past the bolt, then remove the first sling, thus passing the obstruction. *This way you are never unprotected.* Similarly, at the ladders it is clip and climb alternately. Mountaineers, who have climbing harnesses, can obviously use those instead and indeed special *'via ferrata* kits' can sometimes be purchased. Tackling these routes can be good fun, exciting - no wonder they are very popular.

Most famous of all these routes is that which traverses the Brenta Dolomites and is known as the Via delle Bocchette. It is actually a sort of generic name given to ten *vie ferratae* which stretch across the range.

The Brenta Dolomites rise in splendid isolation on the wrong side of the Adige to the Dolomites 'proper'. They are the most westerly Dolomites; facing them across the deep and wooded Valle di Campiglio are the snowy tops of the Adamello-Presanella range. The boundary is startlingly demarcated - there are paths in the valley where the rocks on one side are limestone and on the other granite.

As a group, the Brenta is neat and compact - roughly a north-south ridge of 20km, about half of which, the northern half, is generally forgotten. Most of the interest lies south of the Grosté Pass: here are the towers and pinnacles for which the Brenta is justly famous, including the sensational Campanile Basso, a great rock tower and the Dolomites' ultimate erotic gesture.

The valley base for the Brenta is Madonna di Campiglio, a smart modern village of stainless steel and tinted glass laid in a jewelled setting. It is like a posh version of Chamonix and most of the visitors look as though they have just stepped out of some chic boutique in Milan. Which, indeed, they probably have.

The easiest approach to the ridge is to go up the cable car to Grosté, and so one bright morning a few years ago this is what my son and I did. We had at our disposal only two full days before our return home so we had to select what we hoped would be the best of the Bocchette Way, because to do it all would take a week.

From the pass we followed an easy path threading through a field of limestone blocks. On the horizon the snows of Adamello floated over the heat haze like a white cloud as we appreciated that the start to our adventure was *down!* In no time at all we arrived at the Tuckett Hut, perched on a buttress overlooking the moraines of the Brenta Glacier. Here we had some soup and a drink and then set out to tackle our first *via ferrata*, the SOSAT Weg.

The unusual name for this route comes from abbreviating Sezione Operaia della Societa Alpinisti Tridentini, which proves, if nothing else, that abbreviations have their uses. It led round the head of the moraines to a series of short rock walls where we came across the first of the ladders. These were

short and easy angled, interspersed with the odd length of cable thrown in for good measure, though the going was no harder than, say, Crib Goch in Snowdonia. In a short while we came out above the walls onto an enormous block field where the track threaded its way through limestone boulders comparable in size with a decent garage. It was all good clean fun and the sun was smiling and so were we.

We stopped smiling when we came to the gully. We couldn't believe our eyes. We had squeezed through a curious limestone crevasse and popped out the other

A ladder on the Sentiero SOSAT, a via ferrata in the Brenta Dolomites. A via ferrata is made up of exposed ledges protected by cables and joined by ladders

All the excitement of whitewater rafting is demonstrated in this scene on the Shotover River, Queenstown, New Zealand (Ch 5) *(Courtesy of New Zealand Tourist Board)*

A jetboat skims across Lake Wakatipu at Queenstown, New Zealand. If it is excitement you crave, Queenstown's the place! (Ch 5)

Canadian canoes on the Oulanka River, Finland. Silent forests stretch for miles - and there's gold in the river (Ch 5)

An idyllic camp on the banks of the River Jhelum, in the Vale of Kashmir (Ch 5)

On Wular Lake, Kashmir - a sea of water chestnuts and an island full of hashish! (Ch 5)

Descending to Valdevez and the River Lima in the Penedes-Gêres National Park, Portugal (Ch 5)

Easy walking at Capu Rossu on the Corsican coast (Ch 6)

Few islands can match the dramatic granite scenery of Corsica. This is a view near Creno Lake (Ch 6)

The late Pat Hurley enjoying an ascent of La Coma in Majorca. The Majorcan hills make an excellent introduction to overseas adventure for British hillwalkers (Ch 6)

Pinnacle Rock, Bartolomé Island, with Santiago Island in the background. The volcanic nature of the Galapagos is clearly evident (Ch 6)

Fajazhina on Flores Island in the Azores. The route through the village and across the river proves to be one of the finest coastal walks to be found anywhere (Ch 6)

There is no disguising the volcanic nature of the Azores. These are the hot springs at the aptly named Furnas, São Miguel Island (Ch 6)

end like a couple of jackrabbits, to find ourselves on the brink of an enormous chasm. Across the chasm we could see a ladder bolted to the opposite wall and leading up to what was obviously a path. I say obviously because there was nowhere else it could go, though it was the sort of path our Victorian forefathers with their usual modesty would have described as tenuous. Moreover, the ladder leading up to it was a good hundred feet of vertical ironmongery.

The surprise of the view was so startling that for some time it banished the thought that we first of all had to descend our side of the gully to get to the ladder. The descent turned out to be a complex maze of grooves, cables and ladders threading a way down the wall until eventually it led to an enormous chockstone wedged in the inner recesses of the gully, which continued downwards for a thousand feet. From the chockstone, the great ladder soared upwards.

I have been reliably informed that there are longer ladders in the Dolomites, even in the Brenta, but if so I don't want to meet them. It makes the famous Pas de Chèvres above Arolla look like a set of step ladders. We climbed it conscious of the thousand feet of space below, our sacks dragging us outwards, our palms unduly moist on the iron rungs. At the top was the path with a huge overhang jutting out above it. *Mind your head!* said a notice in several languages.

Once out of the gully all was sweetness and light again. Across from us we could see the Crozzon di Brenta and Cima Tosa, two peaks divided by a great ice couloir. Directly below us, like a doll's house, lay the Brentei Hut. Our own resting place for the night lay a little further on, the Alimonta Hut, perched on a limestone pavement and having 500ft of height advantage over the Brentei.

Our plan next day was to follow the main ridge between two cols known as the Bocca d'Armi and Bocca di Brenta; the very heart of the Bocchette system. It began with a walk up the little glacier leading to the Bocca d'Armi from where the ladders began with brutal immediacy. There was a whole series of them and they landed us on the crest of a narrow neck of rock where the exposure was considerable - and there was no cable! We could only assume that this omission was intended to be a deterrent for the faint-hearted, to make them turn back before it was too late. Balance was a distinct asset at this point but it was only a few feet to the walls of the Torre di Brenta where a good track, and a cable, appeared.

As the ledge led off round the Torre di Brenta we began to appreciate what a *via ferrata* is all about. The way varied from being a broad track over a metre wide to a narrow footledge where the heels of a size nine hung out over space. The common factor was exposure - tremendous, awe-inspiring, sweeping exposure. Yet it was safe enough because we were clipped onto the cable. Just occasionally there were exciting moments when we met parties coming in the opposite direction!

The rock scenery was of unsurpassable grandeur, with the three great spires of the Campanile Alto, Campanile Basso and Brenta Alta dominating everything. Drifts of cloud floated below and around us lending a Wagnerian air to the adventure so that we really felt we were taking a walk with the gods.

At the Sentinella, a minor rocky tooth between the Alto and Basso, the character of the route changed perceptibly. It zig-zagged by cracks and grooves round the side of the Basso and switched from the eastern to the western side of the ridge, giving us dramatic views across deep space to the Crozzon di Brenta. This was actually the crux of the walk, where a nasty gully has to be crossed and we found it needed some delicacy and care since it seemed to consist of huge boulders poised on infinity. But we were soon across it and following an easy ledge towards the Bocca di Brenta. As we strode along we fell in with an old friend, the great Italian guide Cesare Maestri who had been climbing with a client and we chatted about old times until we parted company. Maestri was going down but we were still climbing - up to the col, where we hoped to have a soup and beer at the Tosa Hut. It was not yet mid-day and we were making good time.

The Pedrotti Hut and Tosa Hut form another of those twin hut systems which seem so prevalent in the Dolomites. By force of habit, a lot of climbers still refer to it as the Tosa, which is the older of the two structures, but it is the Pedrotti which is actually in use, with the Tosa a sort of reserve and winter room. Surprisingly, they are quite a distance apart. From our point of view the best feature of the hut was that it gave us a commanding view of our next route, the Sentiero Orsi. It was to be our return route and it looked a doddle.

And so it proved, at least as far as the Naso, where the path rose sharply to a col giving us dramatic views of the great walls of the Croz dell Altissimo, an isolated peak rising out of the woods above Molveno. The Orsi path takes a middle line along the eastern side of the ridge; the Via delle Bocchette - which we had followed that morning - running parallel but high above it. From our stance at the Naso we had a comprehensive view of the central Brenta peaks and it seemed impossible that anyone could find a route up there.

The Sentiero Orsi had so far proved no more difficult than a path in Lakeland, but now it began to fight back. It swung round the cliffs of the Cima Brenta to an ugly looking couloir, filled with jammed boulders. This had to be crossed and turned out to be even nastier than the one we had crossed before lunch - teetering boulders and slippery gravel, with a very big drop below and no safety net. But once that was out of the way the path became a delight and though the mists began to roll in, obscuring our forward view, we knew we couldn't be far from the climb to the Bocca del Tuckett, which was our goal.

Maestri had warned us that the climb to the Tuckett col was very tiring and how right he was! The path vanished in a steep slope of limestone scree which was sheer purgatory. Up and up it went, a never ending treadmill where the rule seemed to be two steps up and one back. It has all the qualities of a Wigan slag heap and made worse by the fact that we couldn't see the top because of the mist. Here and there steel cables were laid on the scree, the idea being to pull yourself up hand over hand as quickly as possible until you could rest and pant for breath in some rocky niche. At the end of a long day it was extremely fatiguing.

But we reached the col at last and on the other side the little Brenta Glacier. We skittered down the ice towards the Tuckett Hut just as the thunder started to roll round the limestone towers. As we stepped into the hut door, the rain began to fall.

SOME FAMOUS LONG DISTANCE WALKS

Here is just a selection of the many long-distance walks available to adventure travellers. All times and distances approximate.

Haute Randonnée Pyrénéenne. France, Spain. 400km. A high level traverse of the Pyrenees. There is a lower and easier alternative, GR10. 44 days

The Way of St James. France, Spain. 1500km approx. From Le Puy to Compostella, the old pilgrim trail. 10/12 weeks

Tour of Mont Blanc. France, Italy, Switzerland. 115km. A circumnavigation of Mt Blanc and its satellites (see Ch 2). 11 days

Corsican High Level Route. 177km The GR20 from Conca to Calenzana across the mountains. Reputed the toughest of the GR walks. 13 days

Tour de la Vanoise. France. 75km. The GR55, an easy tour through the Vanoise National Park. 5 days

Tour of the Oisans. France. 180km. GR54 through the Ecrins National Park. Fairly tough. 10/14 days

Alta Via 1. Italy. 120km. From Lago di Braies to Belluno; the original Dolomite L.D.walk. 7/10 days

The King Ludwig Way. Bavaria. 120km. From Starnberg to Fussen, linking scenes from the life and death of Ludwig, including Neuschwanstein Castle. 5 days

Stubai Rucksack Route. Austria. 120km. Hut to hut through the Stubai Alps. 9 days

The Milford Track, New Zealand. 52km. A popular walk in Fiordland. 5 days.

The Everest Trek. Nepal. 80km from Lukla to Base Camp (see Ch 2). Extremely popular Himalayan trek. 13 days

The Circuit of Annapurna. Nepal. 350km. Spectacular walk round the Annapurna massif. 25/32 days

The Concordia Trek. Pakistan. 100km. A tough mountain trek to the foot of K2. 20 days

The Cordillera Huayhuash Trek. Peru. 166km. A tough circuit of the Huayhuash mountains in the Andes. 11 days

The Inca Trail. Peru. 27km. From Km88 railway station to Machu Picchu; a tough walk through ancient civilization. 4 days

The John Muir Trail. USA. 336km. Through California's mountains from Whitney to Yosemite. 12 days

The Long Trail. USA. 421km. A wooded trail through the Green Mts of Vermont. 15 days

3
Deserts

Mention of deserts conjures up youthful images of Beau Geste and the Foreign Legion or perhaps Lawrence of Arabia charging across the deserts of Jordan with his Bedou, in pursuit of a Turkish army train. Inevitably we imagine sweeping crescent-shaped sand dunes but in fact Scott of the Antarctic has as much right as Lawrence to be thought of as a desert explorer since the great Polar wastes are also technically deserts. But for most people such distinctions are academic - for them the desert means sand, and lots of it.

So it is the dry, hot desert we'll look at in this chapter because that's mostly where adventure trekkers go. True, there are a few trips to the Polar wastes - Antarctica and Spitzbergen are both fairly popular - but the hot deserts are much more widespread and, on the whole, more interesting. They are also cheaper - Antarctic travel tends to be the most expensive of all.

Desert and semi-desert (and it is sometimes difficult to tell them apart) cover a great deal of the Earth. Vast areas of North and South America, Africa, Australia and Asia are arid, with either no vegetation at all or the merest scrub, like tumbleweed and cacti. Most of this land is hard red earth sometimes with a gravel surface, while sometimes the bedrock is laid bare. Here and there sand-seas occur. These seas of sand can be many miles in extent with high dunes, which rest on the underlying earth and move slowly like a great amoeba crawling over the desert's heart.

Water is at a premium, so wells are precious and were once jealously guarded, though perhaps less so nowadays. Sometimes it doesn't rain for years but when it does curious things can happen; I remember camping in the Libyan desert on one occasion when it rained overnight and in the morning the ground was carpeted in lovely flowers like poppies in Picardy. By evening they were all gone again, having lived their brief lives. In the Great Karroo of South Africa a popular expedition is to follow the opening of the spring flowers as the season moves south - here again, a wilderness is transformed into a vivid carpet of colour.

Dry stream beds, known as *wadis* to the Arabs, can quickly become roaring torrents when the rains come. At other times the illusion of water is very common. It appears as a shimmering lake on the horizon; the same sort of thing you can get on a tarmac road during a hot day at home. It is the commonest form of *mirage*, though trees and particularly buildings are quite common too.

If you drive towards them they never come any closer, of course, because they are not really there. The mirage is caused by refraction of light rays in the desert air.

You might think that with such a lack of water, no creatures could live in the desert, but nothing could be further from the truth. Large animals such as gazelle, hyena and even lion are found in the deserts of Asia and Africa, snakes and lizards abound in all deserts and there are many insects. Whilst you are not likely to be bothered by the larger creatures (though I was kept awake one night by a prowling hyena and its frighteningly chilling 'laugh' which sounds like a manic axe-murderer) many of the snakes and insects are poisonous. They generally won't bother you if you don't bother them, but if you come upon one unexpectedly they must have an escape route, or they will attack. They seek shade, so you need to be careful when moving stones, or even clothes which have been left on the ground. If scrambling on desert rocks watch out when reaching into cracks or hidden holds!

Perhaps the creature most dreaded by desert travellers is the scorpion; mostly because its evil nature has come down through age old myths and legends, and because it looks so fearsome, with its stinging tail arched over its back, ready to strike. They are very common, live in holes in the ground and hunt by night, though they rarely need to eat - they can survive for over a year without food and many months without water. Unfortunately they are attracted to human habitation and can lurk in cracks and crevices anywhere - even in bedclothes. They are arachnids, like spiders, live alone and will attack and kill any other scorpion they come across. The female will kill and eat her mate unless he gets out of the way quickly. Scorpions vary in size from about 1cm to 18cm, but there is such a wide variation within a single species that they are not always easy to identify. This is unfortunate because some are much more poisonous than others. Some of the most fearsome looking ones are relatively harmless but beware the pale green or yellow ones, even if quite small. The effects of the milder stings wear off in a couple of hours, though the more dangerous sorts can last for ten hours, are often very painful and can only be treated in hospital. Deaths occur, usually only to small children - however, it is worth noting that world-wide there are more deaths from scorpion stings than from snake bites.

Funnily enough, some animals - gerbils and guinea pigs, for instance - are immune to scorpion stings. Scorpions themselves can be victims - I once saw a scorpion attacked by ants who quickly overcame it, dissected it and carried off the pieces for lunch.

Swanning - travelling in the Western Desert of Libya

I first navigated in the desert many years ago whilst doing my National Service in Libya. We would take a small truck or a jeep and go off into the desert from our base at Benghazi, ostensibly investigating something or other, such as whether a new radio would work (almost invariably it didn't). We called it *swanning*, because we 'swanned off' into the desert, beyond the reach of authority. Fortunately this is what we were paid to do, so everyone was satisfied.

It was quite easy to get lost because the map consisted of a blank sheet with just a few wells or *bir* marked and a rough indication of where there might be a track. A few years previous, of course, it had been one of the most famous battlegrounds of World War II, where Rommel and Montgomery chased one another over the sand. A good deal of war-time detritus remained, lost or simply forgotten about and it is probably still there. Thousands of shells in their cases, abandoned by their gunners, knocked out tanks by the dozen but probably the most eerie discovery we made was a Spitfire fighter plane, tipped up on its nose with a bent propeller, but otherwise in perfect condition. What had happened to the pilot? He must have got out and walked off. The nearest habitation was 200 miles away. I hope he made it.

We would often drive in from the coast, past the desert village of Solluch and up the great escarpment by the Esc Schledeima Pass with its ruined

The ancient city of Cyrene in Libya, approached from the so-called Pilgrims' Way

Turkish fort, like something from Beau Geste, into the 'blue', or desert proper. Only the merest scrub existed here, amidst the gravel and red earth. Before we had travelled many miles our faces would be red with the desert dust, except where our goggles had protected our eyes. When we removed the goggles we looked like red pandas. Rain could turn the surface into a quagmire of red mud,

The Temple of Apollo at Cyrene in Libya. Simon of Cyrene carried the Cross for Jesus, and the city is an idyllic site between desert and sea

but even in winter it didn't rain often. The main enemy was the sun and I soon learned that to be fair haired or red haired meant you suffered agonies of sunburn. We had no sunblock so we learned to protect ourselves in every possible way - we envied those Foreign Legion *kepis*, but made do with a white hanky stuffed under the beret and covering the neck.

One day a few of us were driving near the desert crossroads of Zaviet Msus when a sandstorm blew up out of nowhere. In seconds we were enveloped in a thick cloud of swirling dust and it was quite impossible to see where we were going. We ground to a halt. All we could do was to sit out the ferocious wind. Sand got into everything. Fortunately we were in a truck and fairly protected but in a jeep it could have been serious, for when I tried to climb out of the truck it felt as though a savage rasp was being drawn across my bare face and arms and I hurried back into shelter. It seemed to go on for hours but it was probably less than an hour really and it died away as suddenly as it had begun. When we climbed out it was to discover than all the corners and knobbly bits on the truck has been sandpapered clear of paint.

The Western Desert is that part of Libya known as Cyrenaica and there is much to see there, because besides the desert itself there are the coastal hills of the Jebel Ahkdar, which means green mountains, with their deep sandstone ravines such as the Wadi Kuf which has sheer rock walls of 500ft or more, the cave-tombs of Tocra, where you could still pick up Roman coins in the sand, and the lovely coast at Derna. Derna is where the US Marines landed in 1805 to crush the infamous Barbary pirates and hence their battle-song 'to the

Wadi Rum in Jordan is now a centre for desert expeditions. Climbers tackle the huge sandstone walls of the gorge

shores of Tripoli'. Above all there are the ruins of Cyrene, home of Simon, who carried the cross for Jesus, you may recall; a superb sweep of Greek and Roman temples tumbling down towards the sea and one of the most impressive sites of the ancient world.

Under present day political circumstances Cyrenaica is a difficult option for the adventurous traveller but at least one company runs trips there (see Appendix 1).

I have always thought it a paradox that deserts, the most desolate places on earth, are also the places where you can find remains of the greatest civilizations. If it is awesome ruins you are after forget Rome or Athens and go instead to the great desert lands - what Shelley wonderfully described in *Ozymandias* as 'an antique land'. The folly of presumed immortality is everywhere. There are lots of 'trunkless legs of stone', lots of 'shattered visages' and, as in the poem:

> *Nothing beside remains. Round the decay*
> *Of that colossal wreck, boundless and bare*
> *The lone and level sands stretch away.*

Perhaps it is the setting that makes these ruins seem all the greater - Cyrene stretching down from the desert to the azure blue Mediterranean, the secret rocky desert defile of glorious Petra in Jordan or the many ruins in Egypt's sands. There is a romance about these places, and none more so than the vast horizons of Central Asia, where the hordes of Genghis Khan created instant ruins wherever they went and where the equally savage Tamerlane created some of the most glorious buildings of the ancient world.

In the Steps of Genghis Khan

The deserts of the Middle East and Central Asia, dominated by the world of Islam, contain some of the finest sites of antiquity. Those which are easily accessible, like the ruins of Petra in the Jordan valley, have long been popular tourist places, though there's adventure to be found in the treks now available from Wadi Rum, where a new rest-house has been established. The soaring red sandstone walls of Rum have to be seen to be believed. But you are never too far from civilisation in Jordan and the adventure is muted. For more serious fare you need to visit Central Asia.

Since the break up of the old Soviet republics it has become much easier to penetrate into Central Asia and it had long been an ambition of mine to cross the fabled Oxus River to reach Merv, the heart of old Asia, the jewel of the Silk Road and the scene of Genghis Khan's greatest carnage. My route led me on the golden road to Samarkand, that most romantically named of ancient cities, which is now becoming almost as popular with tourists as Petra and, lovely though the blue tiled city of Tamerlane is, I was anxious to push further out, to Bukhara, Khiva and, hopefully, Merv.

The great walled city of Bukhara is a wonderful jewel, set in the desert. In the last century its rulers were notoriously cruel, and you can still see the flea pit in which the British officers Conolly and Stoddart were imprisoned before their execution and climb the great Tower of Death from which unfortunate victims were flung. It is a place of mysterious alleys, covered markets and a multitude of ancient mosques and *madrassehs* - the colleges where Islamic law and religion are taught. During the Soviet era the Mini Arab Madrasseh was the only permitted college for Moslem priests in the whole of Soviet Asia. The ancient town with its crumbling mud walls has none of the grandeur of Samarkand, but is a more interesting place.

Exodus Travel had hired a bus to take our little group from Samarkand to Bukhara and beyond. The roads were surprisingly good and along the way, quite apart from the famous cities, there was plenty of evidence that this was indeed 'an antique land'. The great underground tank at Rabat-i-Malik was still holding water after 500 years and near Navoi some unknown hills had a gorge carved with ancient rock art, very similar to that of the African bushmen. How long it had been there or what peoples had done it, nobody seemed to

Inside a yurt in Central Asia. Traditional hospitality dictates that food and drink be served even to passing strangers

know. We climbed out of the gorge and walked back to the bus over some hills reminiscent of the Derbyshire moors. It was a wild, magical moment to stand on the tops and look out over Central Asia. We felt we were discovering the unknown; had any others been before us? *Hassan* came to mind again:

> *For the lust of knowing what should not be known,*
> *We take the Golden Road to Samarkand.*

Bukhara itself was a delight but we were determined to press on and cross the River Oxus to the town of Urgench. It was a long drive through miles of semi-desert but on the way we called at a lonely *yurt*, mainly because the bus had broken down. A *yurt* is a dome-like tent stretched over a frame and it served as home to a farmer and his family. The owner was delighted to see us and his wife fussed about, insisting on providing simple refreshment, while grandfather held the baby. The place was fitted with cheap rugs (real Bukhara rugs are expensive, even in Bukhara!) and a crockery cupboard. The farmer told us he looked after 600 karakol sheep (the animal from which astrakhan is made) of which 80 were his and the rest belonged to a collective. How they managed to live off the sparse scrub was a mystery.

At last we reached the Oxus, or Amu Darya, which proved to be a swift flowing, wide river of grey silt-filled water crossed by a surprisingly large car ferry like a great flat barge. It was a disappointingly unromantic crossing, perhaps, for one of the most romantic rivers in the world, for the Oxus is a river of mystery and legend. For over 1500 miles it flows through the very heart of Central Asia and to cross the Oxus is a milestone in any traveller's career.

That night we arrived in Urgench, an unlovely town, like so many built during the Soviet era, but on the following day we drove the short distance to ancient Khiva; at one time regarded as one of the most mysterious places on earth, equalling Lhasa or Timbuctoo in that respect. In fact, the present town isn't all that old - a century or so - but the heart of it has been lovingly restored so that it forms a perfect 19th-century Central Asian city, walled about and containing palaces and mosques in exquisite forms. Perhaps that is the problem - Khiva, the last khanate to fall to the Russians during the heady days of the Great Game in 1873, is almost too perfect, like a Disney theme park. I much preferred the rough and tumble of old Bukhara. A couple of us wandered away from the usual places and found the ruined south gate of the old town; here the walls had not been restored, the gate not tarted up. That's more like it!

Although we had reached Khiva, our journey was far from over. The next stage was to reach ancient Merv and this involved crossing the Kara Kum desert. The name means the 'desert of black sand' but in fact it was yellow sand and endless scrub, stretching to the horizon. It was a very long journey along a neglected narrow road across which the sand drifted in places. According to most atlases the road doesn't exist. Here and there we came across abandoned buildings, like the old wartime control towers which once dotted the airfields of Britain and we reckoned they had something to do with natural gas exploration, though nobody seemed to know, not even our Uzbek guides.

It was very late when we arrived at Mary, the modern replacement for Merv and another unlovely Stalinist city. We had crossed the border into Turkmenistan from Uzbekistan, each now a separate state. We were stopped by the police four times as we entered the town; young kids mostly, whom we bribed with biros to avoid lengthy examination of our travel documents and passports. The journey across the Kara Kum had been exhausting and we were in no mood for lengthy explanations, though excited at the prospect of the morrow.

And the next day we visited Merv, fount of our ambitions and hopes. Merv is another landmark for an ambitious traveller. This was once the greatest city in Central Asia, a rival to Baghdad, and the reputed home of both Zarathustra and Scheherezade. A million people lived here, but in 1221 the Mongol hordes under Genghis Khan's youngest son Toloi swept down on Merv, razed it to the ground and massacred the inhabitants. It was the Mongol's bloodiest slaughter - and that's saying a lot.

Though the city was rebuilt several times it never regained its supremacy. Undiscerning travellers have failed to see what there is about the place that is so exciting because it remains very much as the Mongols left it - a wasteland of ruins, covering hundreds of acres with the huge mausoleum of Sultan Sanjar and the gaunt walls of the Kys Kala palace, all fluted and pebbled, rising above the devastation. The ancient fort that was the heart of the city is just a great mound of ochre earth now. As a scene of utter desolation Merv has been compared with Hiroshima after the bomb and I suppose the Mongol horde *was* the atom bomb of its day. I was strangely affected - it was as if I could hear the screams of a million dying people . It is an intensely moving sight.

As the sun went down, bathing the scene in blood, a small but intensely poisonous snake wriggled past us. It seemed symbolic, somehow.

After Merv we continued our travels to the Turkmen capital of Ashkabad, rebuilt after the devastating earthquake of 1948 which killed 110,000 people. Nowadays it is famous for its Sunday carpet market, where hundreds of old and new Bukhara carpets are laid out to view, covering acres of the desert in gaudy reds. It is a lively, crowded scene and apparently carpet buyers from all over the world come to do business here, but on the Sunday we were there we were the only westerners to be seen. We discovered that not only could you buy a carpet, you can buy yourself a camel on which to carry it away!

Not far from Ashkabad we drove to another ancient city - Central Asia is full of them - called Nisac, once the capital of the mighty Parthian empire, whose horsemen could swivel round in the saddle to fire arrows, even when in retreat - hence 'the parting shot', which is a corruption of 'the Parthian shot'. Excavations were under way. The site was much more compact than Merv, though not nearly as fascinating. Very little of Merv has been excavated; it's a lifetime job for somebody.

But you cannot travel these deserts of Central Asia for far without coming across the scene of yet another bloody massacre. The land is soaked in the blood of centuries. Not far from Nisac are the remains of the Turkmen fort at Geok Tepe, where in 1879 a Russian expedition was routed by the tribesmen and the Czar humiliated. But not for long. The following year he sent General Skobelev with 11,000 troops to wreak revenge and after a month of skirmishing the Russians managed to blow a hole in the walls and poured in, slaughtering 20,000 of their enemy. "I wanted to make sure that when I knocked them down they would never get up again", the general said. They never did, but news of the massacre raised an international outcry and Skobelev was sent home in disgrace where he died shortly after in a Moscow brothel.

Not surprisingly in view of past events, neither the Soviets, when they were in charge, nor the present regime, are anxious to allow visitors into the site of the old fort, but by a bit of wangling we managed it - perhaps the first westerners to see it. There's nothing left now but some large and ominous mounds and a few bones sticking out of the earth.

All pleasures have their costs. The trip through Central Asia was a wonderful experience which I wouldn't have missed for the world, but it did have a down side. I had the worst dysentery I have ever experienced. Tummy trouble is common in most hot countries and a recent survey reveals about a third of all travellers experience it. It is often given names like Delhi Belly, the Kathmandu Quickstep and Montezuma's Revenge. It can be very debilitating and very distracting too because it is hard to keep your mind on the architectural marvels of an ancient temple when you are wondering where the nearest loo is situated. Public loos, which in Asia are universally disgusting, can become objects of desire! Long distance bus travel can be a nightmare.

The milder form of diarrhoea is usually caused by a change of diet. We all have bugs permanently in our stomachs, but our bugs are not their bugs and so when we ingest some local bug it upsets us, whereas the locals are used to it. Maybe *they* would have the same reaction to fish and chips, I can't say.

The usual advice given to travellers is to avoid this and that - but it can be very difficult, if not impossible. However, for what it is worth, avoid salads, and fruit you can't peel, ice in drinks and, of course, the local water supply. Well cooked food should be the order of the day and in my experience Chinese cooking, in the wok, is best. I have eaten at some very grubby roadside cafes in China and never suffered at all and I believe this is due to the food being fresh and freshly cooked as you wait. It is not something I would do in an Indian street booth!

A Chinese public lavatory near the Burma Road in Yunnan. Despite its exotic architecture, this was no less disgusting than most Asian lavatories

Diarrhoea is dehydrating so it is necessary to drink plenty of water, preferably laced with electrolyte such as Isostar. The problem here is that the water may well be the chief cause of the trouble

A handy little water filter
(photo: Camping Gaz Ltd.)

and so it has to be purified. Nowadays this can be done by portable filters, provided they are able to remove bacteria larger than 0.5uM. The model I use is called PUR which combines two methods: a microfilter removes organisms of 1.0uM (such as giardia) then an iodine resin kills smaller bacteria and viruses on contact. There are other types which will turn virtual sludge into drinking water, at a price. None of the filters will desalinate, incidentally.

Alternatively you can sterilize the water with iodine tablets, remembering that you need to give it time to work - the colder the water the longer it takes, up to 20 minutes. Iodine should not be used over an extended period and not at all if you have thyroid problems when chlorine tablets can be used instead, though they are not as effective.

Most effective of all is to boil the water for at least two minutes plus extra time for altitude. Water boils at 1°C less for every 300m of height, but the bugs won't be killed at under 70°C, which means you can just about get away with it on top of Everest!

Water is such an everyday thing in the west that it is easy to forget precautions - ice in drinks (some bugs like alcohol as much as you do), cleaning teeth, washing food under infected water and so on. Tea is better than instant coffee simply because, as mentioned, the water needs to be boiled for tea, but not for coffee. Soft drinks are safe in cans, but there is a risk with bottles bought from a street vendor. I have seen bottles being refilled at the stall, and caps replaced! Similarly with bottled water - you need to ensure that it is in a properly sealed bottle, not merely a capped and certainly not a screw top bottle. When in doubt - filter.

Faecal contamination is one of the prime causes of diarrhoea because it gets into the water and food is prepared and eaten with hands not as clean as they should be. Hands must be washed even if the local water is a bit suspect - use plenty of soap or put some Dettol in the water. In some eastern hotels 'drinking water' is provided in a bedroom flask and this could be used for washing hands. I don't think I'd use it for drinking!

Mild diarrhoea should clear itself in a day or two but more persistent kinds may need Ciproxin. Worse still is giardia, caused by a parasitic protozoa, and now spread to many regions of the world and even present in some public water supplies. Pain, frequent wind, recurrent and foul smelling diarrhoea are all symptoms. The treatment is Flagyl. If you are going to eastern countries the use of Ciproxin and Flagyl should be discussed with your doctor before setting out.

But what about the ever useful Lomotil or Imodium; the travellers' standby? These drugs are not cures - indeed just the opposite, because they are blockers which prevent the toxic agents being flushed out. They paralyse the bowels - and so they are useful on journeys when going to the loo is not possible. But they should be used sparingly and never, under any circumstances, given to children.

Needless to say, if medical advice is available it should be sought and any traveller who has suffered particularly badly whilst abroad should have a check up on his or her return to this country.

The Spelunca Gorge in Corsica (Ch 7)

For a few yards of doubt and indecision the Virgin River Narrows Route in Zion Canyon, Utah, involves wading chest deep (Ch 7)

The Sentier Martel gives spectacular views into the Verdon Gorge, France (Ch 7)

Looking back from Point Sublime to the Samson Corridor of the Verdon Gorge, France (Ch 7)

Following the North Kaibab Trail into Grand Canyon (Ch 7)

Descending into the Yangtze Gorge near Baoshan. This part of the Yangtze is virtually unknown to outsiders (Ch 7)

Flowers are a feature of many adventure trips and there are tours which specialise in them. Cistus flowers cover Capu Rossu in spring, Corsica (Appendix 1)

Animals and birds are the subject of many special tours. Here is a land iguana on Plaza Island in the Galapagos (Appendix 1)

A camera can make unique records of unforgettable moments like this on the Dal Lake in Kashmir (Appendix 2)

Goodbye, New York! Passengers on the QE2 leave the Big Apple and the picture shows the superb resolution of a modern compact camera which can be carried in the pocket - in this case a Minolta Riva Zoom 105EX (Appendix 2)

4

Forests and Jungles

Although many of the world's forests, especially hardwood forests, are under attack as never before there are still many thousands of square miles virtually unknown to man and the preserve of bear and tiger. Even where they have been explored by local natives and the traditional trails recognized they can still be dangerous places for the traveller. In really thick forest or jungle a local guide is essential.

Paradoxically, too, much forest trekking can be boring. A friend and I once walked part of the Long Trail, a 425km route which traverses the Green Mountains of Vermont to the Canadian border. It is one of the oldest long-distance trails, being established as long ago as 1910, but apart from exciting bits like the ascent of the Camel's Hump or Mount Mansfield, which were satisfyingly steep and rocky, the walk was without much merit. I remember one day when we set off walking through the forest at 8 in the morning and by 5 at night we might just as well have been in the same place! Nothing had changed all day; just trees and more trees.

Not that Vermont is entirely without interest. In the 'fall' the forests turn every shade from deep green to deep purple with glowing oranges and fiery reds in between; a remarkable display of nature. This is the season when the 'leaf-peepers', as the locals call them, come out by their droves from Boston and New York to stay at the celebrated New England inns - marvellous institutions combining tradition and good food. If walking is confined to mountains such as those mentioned above or shorter trails like the little Deer Leap Trail, there's much to interest the adventurer. I remember on Mount Mansfield scrambling up the various trails that have been worked out including the exposed trail known as Subway because at one stage it dives underground. On the summit a young woman asked how we had got up and when I told her she decided to go and do it. "It's quite exciting", I assured her. "You'll enjoy it." So off she went. My companion looked at me disapprovingly. "I do wish you would stop sending people to their deaths," he said.

I once flew north from Helsinki over the heart of Finland towards the Arctic Circle. Looking down it seemed as though the whole country was an endless carpet of forest. Hundreds of lakes glittered like silver mirrors amongst the dark trees. We landed at Kuusamo and went for a short walk in the woods, though most of our time was spent on the lakes and rivers (see Ch 5). A good

The ascent of Mount Mansfield makes a welcome break in the interminable forests of Vermont

deal of the forest here is *taiga*, that is, trees growing in swamp conditions, and there is a multi-day walk here called the Bears' Ring which explores this.

There are very few bears now in Finland's forests but they are pretty active elsewhere and must be guarded against. Normally they will clear off if they hear you coming and I have at times adopted the precaution of tapping tree trunks and stones with my stick and deliberately snapping twigs underfoot - whether this was effective, I can't say, but I never saw any bears. In America the ones to watch out for are grizzlies which are tan coloured with a blond collar and a hump at the neck; brown and black bears are not as fearsome, but all bears are dangerous to a degree, and especially if it's a mother with young. Most injuries are caused by bears with young. If you meet a grizzly the recommended action is to climb a tree (grizzlies can't climb) or play dead, which sounds to me like something good in theory but damn difficult in practice! Some national parks have 'tame' bears and people try to be photographed with them - but just keep in mind that there is really no such thing as a tame bear. You can't outrun a bear, and they actually run faster uphill than down!

You are more likely to have bear trouble at night if you are camping (even in relatively popular places like Yosemite) because the bears will sniff out any food you have. A tent is no protection, so the thing to do is make sure that all food is placed in stuffsacks or rucksacks out of harm's way - usually hung from a branch out of reach. Plates should be cleaned and no scraps of food left near the tent. (Other animals such as raccoons will try to steal food too. Many American national parks provide hanging poles to keep food out of the way of temptation.)

In most temperate forests the greatest handicap is the midge and its various relatives such as mosquitoes, sandflies, no-see-ums and the like. All are irritating

Walking through the taiga forest of northern Finland

but in my experience the nastiest by far is the New Zealand sandfly, especially on the West Coast of South Island. When they bite, they leave an irritating and long lasting mark which no amount of anti-bite cream seems to cure. Anti-histamine tablets help. Some bugs, like the sandfly, are only active during the day, others are nocturnal. There is nothing for it but to douse yourself in a repellent containing Deet (diethyltoluamide) and keep as much flesh covered as possible. There is a device called a head net, made of repellent impregnated netting, which fits over a hat and keeps the little devils away from your face, much the same as bee-keepers wear against bees. During the night a mosquito net hung over the bed is useful. It too should be impregnated with repellent.

In the tropics, of course, the chief danger is from malarial mosquitoes and as well as the preventive measures above, the appropriate malarial tablets have to be taken. If you are going to a malarial zone it is as well to check out *some weeks in advance* which prophylactic is recommended for the area. This is not necessarily a simple matter - you may not need the same protection for, say, sophisticated Singapore as you do for the jungle in nearby Malaysia. As the mosquitoes build up resistance to a drug, too, so the situation changes but remember that up to the minute advice can be got from the Medical Advisory Service for Travellers Abroad MASTA (see Introduction).You normally have to start a course of malaria tablets well in advance and continue it for some weeks after your return. Unfortunately some newer anti-malarial drugs can have unpleasant side effects for some people, though not everybody. This is another reason for starting on the drugs early, to discover your reactions to them and discuss any effects with your doctor. The sad fact is that no anti-malarial drug is completely efficacious these days as different strains grow resistant to medicines.

In recent years the word 'jungle' seems to have fallen into disfavour. Nowadays it is all 'tropical rainforests', which makes it sound much more comfortable and obviously worth protecting. Nevertheless, the jungle is still the jungle and no amount of political correctness will change it. It is still hot, humid, incredibly difficult to travel through and full of some of the most beautiful, not to mention some of the most fearsome, things on God's earth. Fortunately most of the latter will try to avoid you.

The first brief encounter I had with a jungle was most disappointing. It was the Amazon jungle along the banks of the Madre de Dios River, on which stands the gold-mining town of Puerto Maldonado, which looks like the last place on earth and where the airport reception is a tin shed with a shop selling nothing but Brazil nuts - you could get a whole sackful for a dollar. We sailed up the river to a research station, where they were studying jungle life, and we expected a hot and sticky journey, instead of which it turned out to be extremely cold and I was forced to put on my duvet jacket to keep warm. Fortunately, I'd been in the Andes, so was carrying all my cold weather gear. But when I tell people I wore a duvet for a trip up the Amazon, I get funny looks.

It continued cold at the research station, as a result of which all the exotic animals we had come to see had promptly gone to earth, hiding in the warmest places they could find. "Only two days ago," wailed one of the researchers, looking at an empty patch of grass, "there was a huge anaconda there!" We didn't know whether to be glad or sorry.

But why was it so cold? Well, apparently every so often there is a sudden temperature inversion and the cold air from the Andes comes sweeping down while the hot, light air from the jungle blows away. Unfortunately for us we had picked just such a season.

It was on this river that we went crocodile catching; a much overrated sport. It is done at night in canoes. Across the dark surface of the river the native guide shines a torch and dozens of bright lights blink back like cats' eyes on a crazy road. They are crocs' eyes. The guide paddles the boat over to a pair, then reaching into the water, snatches a croc up triumphantly, shows it round the boat then puts it back in the water. Of course, it is a very tiny croc. Even so, visitors are not allowed to take part, because even small crocs can give a nasty nip!

Anywhere that is hot and sticky is likely to be a home for leeches, a creature most people find repugnant even to think about. There are many kinds of leeches, varying in length from less than an inch to several inches. Some are brightly coloured. Some live in streams and lakes, others on land. It is these last that concern us - they are common throughout tropical Asia, and the islands of the Pacific and Indian oceans, and are the true bloodsuckers. They are generally quite small and can squirm through the smallest orifices such as boot laceholes and knitted garments. They congregate near trails on grass, bushes and trees, waiting for passing humans or other creatures. Prey is detected by various sensations like ground movement, shadows and smell. Their bite is painless and once they have had their fill of blood, which extends them to many times their original size, they drop off. They only eat once a year.

No attempt should be made to pull them off because they will simply leave their heads behind and sepsis will result. They can be removed by the traditional methods of touching them with a lighted cigarette or with salt, but since few people smoke nowadays and not many carry salt around with them these remedies are not really practical. I have found that the best thing to make them drop off is one of those ammonia pencils sold as an antidote to insect bites and easily obtained at the chemists and carried in a pocket. A drop of ammonia near the leech's head is very effective. However, prevention is better than cure and though nothing will keep all the leeches off, tobacco is a good remedy, recommended to me by a guide in Borneo. Simply put shredded tobacco in your socks and smear it on other hidden parts where you think the little devils may get - it works!

I once asked a guide what to do about leeches and he said "Learn to love 'em". Well, that's hard advice to follow, but in fact leeches do no harm. They don't hurt you and they do not spread disease - not even HIV. As far as I know, nobody ever died of a leech bite. I wouldn't like to lie wounded in the jungle though…

In the jungle perhaps more than elsewhere, awareness is essential. You must keep your wits about you and exercise constant vigilance. This will prevent most of the bad things than can happen - even leeches can be reduced by being careful not to brush continually against shrubs and branches.

Forest and jungle varies enormously depending on where it is situated. Some of the most impenetrable are the rainforests of New Zealand where there are exotic ferns and shrubs that look like living fossils left over from prehistoric times. They have sharp thorns and spikes in many cases and must be amongst the most unfriendly plants in the world. The early gold prospectors of South Island's West Coast had a terrible time trying to struggle to their diggings. On the other hand there are no wild animals, snakes, leeches or other nasties, except the terrible sandflies.

There are wild animals in the forests which clothe the lower slopes of Mount Kilimanjaro in Tanzania: elephant, buffalo, rhino, leopards and monkeys. Even though the trees are reminiscent of a Surrey woods, it probably wouldn't be wise to stray off the track. I remember one night staying at the Mandara Hut, which rests in a forest clearing, and listening to the cacophony of noise coming from the trees - it sounded like a riot in a zoo. As you climb up the mountain the jungle suddenly gives way to slopes of heathland with giant lobelias dotted about like something from another planet. On Mount Kinabalu in Sabah, where it rains heavily every day, the jungle stretches up to within a couple of thousand feet of the summit and as it does so changes character, from lush tropical jungle to gnarled and twisted trees in the Alpine zone. There are some wonderful flowers, including giant rhododendrons and rare orchids.

A Walk in the Bush - Kruger National Park, South Africa

Bush country is different again. Shrubs and stunted trees, with little undergrowth, is the norm and it is often easy to move through it, though your shirt might be plucked by the thorn bushes, graphically known in South Africa as the 'wait-a-bit' bush. I once spent a fascinating week-end walking through the Kruger National Park in South Africa in the company of a couple of rangers, called Swanee and Enos - one white and one black. It was a great privilege because normally only the rangers are allowed to *walk* in the park - everyone else must stay in their cars, windows up, until they reach one of the park centres like Skukuza which is securely fenced off from the bush and the animals which lurk there. But several times a year certain week-ends are available for bush walk-abouts - places on these trips are limited and you have to book a long time in advance. You sleep the night in a prepared *lager*: safari tents surrounded by a thick thorn fence with a bright fire crackling in the centre of the compound. Outside I could hear a large animal grunting and growling as it padded round and round the fence - a leopard, the ranger said, though it was too dark to see.

During the day we walked through the bush, acutely aware that this was alien territory and that we were not alone. Each ranger carried a pistol and a heavy Winchester rifle and we all walked single file like an army patrol with a ranger at the head and rear of the column. The guns were for safety, of course, but according to Swanee only one animal had ever been shot - a charging rhino. We visited a water hole where crocodiles sunned themselves on the banks and then followed a dried up river bed where we came across the bare bones of a giraffe, laid out in exemplary fashion as if in a natural history museum. It must simply have laid down and died.

The giraffes astonished me with their camouflage; they stand stock still in the trees and you can almost stumble over them, they are so well hidden. Herds of springbok drifted through the bush, frightened at the least movement we made. Buffalo and especially rhinos were common and we were wary of both. There were other animals too: "Did you see the lions?" said a warden we bumped into on his patrol.

"No," we said.

"Well, they've seen you," he said with a grin. "They've been following you for ten minutes - six of 'em"

Towards evening we climbed up to a rock *kopje* to watch the sun go down. In a cave in the rocks there were Bushmen paintings. They could have been a thousand years old - or perhaps only ten; there is no way of telling.

Cone Rock- A day on the West Coast of South Island, New Zealand

If you've never been bitten by a New Zealand sandfly, you don't know what biting is. Scottish midges seem positively amateurish by comparison and if you have never had to struggle through a rainforest on South Island's West Coast in a tropical downpour, you have one of life's more memorable experiences awaiting you.

So why were we struggling through a West Coast rainforest in a teeming downpour, and being bitten by sandflies? I remember thinking that if this wasn't Purgatory it was a damn good working model for it. This is because New Zealand rainforests are full of thrashing ferns about ten feet high and spiky plants that are very nasty at close quarters. Fortunately there is no unpleasant livestock; no bears, snakes, leeches or red-back spiders, only the sandflies which do their best to make up for the rest.

We should not have been struggling through the undergrowth at all. Our little group had set out on a simple stroll from Fox Glacier Village to view the glacier itself from the Chalet Lookout; a thousand feet or so of gentle ascent and a round trip of 5 miles. It was meant to be an easy day in view of the poor weather but we thought it would be superior to the tourist route up the other side of the valley. According to the map half the journey could actually be done by car, because a metalled highway called Glacier View Road ran up towards the Chalet, presumably to help in stocking the hut which once looked out over the ice. But a barrier across the road stopped us before we had even started. The road beyond had totally collapsed and a hundred yards of crumpled tarmac lay in the stream, far below. Shame about the Toyota caught on the wrong side.

And so we had to make a by-pass; to thrash through the rainforest until we could rejoin the road. It wasn't easy, what with the rain and the flies and the spiky vegetation, but as soon as we were out of the difficulties and onto the road again it stopped raining, though the skies remained leaden grey and an air of damp depression hung over the surrounding trees. We trudged up the road until it ended in a redundant parking space, giving way to a rocky path. Once again the trees closed in. In single file we pushed through the wet foliage, following the narrow path, but at least there was a proper path this time and the going was easy. A couple of wide streams, ribbons of rushing water, added excitement to the walk as we waded across them, and before long we were at the Lookout, peering over the cliff edge at the distant glacier. Like most glaciers, this one had retreated.

I can't say it was a thrilling sight. The sky was grey, the ice was grey, the moraine was grey and the mountains were darker grey. It would have delighted Whistler's paintbrush. I took some photographs and wondered why I had colour in the camera.

As we turned for home, Mark, our guide, suggested we might like to return via Cone Rock, a variation that would give us some more monochromatic views of the glacier, but from a higher vantage point. It involved a little scrambling, he explained, but nothing that experienced chaps like us couldn't handle. Just follow the fixed ropes and ladders… oh, and keep a sharp lookout for places where the path might have fallen a thousand feet to the moraines. Otherwise there were no problems. He declined to accompany us.

Cone Rock is only really apparent when you are standing on the moraines of the Fox Glacier, from which it rises as a sheer cliff hundreds of feet high, vaguely cone shaped, liberally covered in scrub and marked by a huge scar where a great slice has fallen away. From where we stood near the Chalet Lookout, Cone Rock was nothing but a swelling in the rainforest, but once we started on the path to it, the steepness became rapidly apparent.

The path was narrower than before and hemmed in by the dripping forest. It obviously wasn't much used these days; any popularity it once might have had disappearing with changing fashions, especially when parts of the upper path collapsed to the moraines below. It soon turned into a scramble over moss covered boulders, wet and greasy. It was exhausting work and for once I found my trekking pole a nuisance as I balanced and slithered on the rocks. It was even more of a nuisance when we came to the crags - short climbs of 15 or 20 feet equipped with skimpy iron ladders or sometimes 'ropes', made of something akin to old-fashioned lavatory chain. The chain cut into my hands abominably but the rock was wet and greasy and I was forced to cling on while my boots slithered in all directions.

At last we reached the first and only surviving of the three lookouts for which Cone Rock is celebrated. The others had joined the glacier a thousand feet below. The view was splendid, but we still had far to go, steeply up to the summit (what was left of it) then down, incredibly steeply, by boulder and gully to the main path far below.

No sooner had we passed the top than the rain started in earnest again, adding to our misery. The rock became more slippery than ever and in descending some tree roots I managed the incredible feat of twisting my foot, my leg and my stick in one sickening jolt. It was shortly after this that we came across the Davie Balfour steps - I call them this because they reminded me of the incident in *Kidnapped* where Davie's wicked uncle sends him up some steps in the dark and only a fortuitous flash of lightning reveals that the steps end in space. Incredible though it may seem, someone had built a short flight of concrete steps in the middle of the rainforested slopes - but the lower end finished hanging in space, a drop of a dozen feet or so where the land had washed away. Anyone galloping down the steps in relief would come to a nasty finish. Other bits of steps appeared, all dilapidated and we realized Cone Rock must have been a favourite place for the guides to bring adventurous tourists in days gone by, like those grottoes in the Alps where wooden walkways were constructed over deep gorges and formed an exciting day out for the Cook's tourists.

Gradually the descent became less steep and we stumbled across the abandoned road. The rain still poured down like glass rods, more obvious on the open road out of the forest's shelter. Past the forlorn Toyota, doomed to remain in limbo, and back through the jungle to Fox Glacier Village and a much needed beer.

The Headhunters' Trail - Through the jungles of Borneo

B orneo is the third largest island in the world after Greenland and New Guinea and is almost entirely covered in dense tropical jungle. The temperature often hovers in the high 80s °F (20°-31°C) and since the rainfall is heavy the humidity is high; hot and sticky describes Borneo for most of the time. No wonder the vegetation is so lush.

The towns and roads, such as they are, stick more or less to the coast or the river banks. Inland, jungle covered mountains predominate and one of them, Kinabalu, pokes free of the trees in a series of stark pinnacles and crags which are the highest in SE Asia. It is incredibly difficult country to travel, which is why great use is made of the many rivers. Until the arrival of light aircraft, rivers were the only means of transport in Borneo.

In the old days nobody went into the jungle except to hunt. The inhabitants, called Dyaks, would hunt the wild pig for food, and each other for a more grisly trophy - human heads. This was the head-hunting capital of the world

The landing at Long Letut on the Melinau River in Borneo

and undertaken with fanatical fervour, especially by the Iban tribe, who were the most numerous. Before a young Iban warrior could marry he had to present his bride with thirteen severed heads. That's known as having a head start!

Inter-tribal raids were common and certain tracks through the jungle became trade routes. One of these has become the basis for an adventurous jungle trek which also includes the great caves of Mulu. Our party organised by Explore was led on this occasion by James Wan, himself an Iban with a university degree - his grandfather actually used this trail in earnest!

Our trip began from the little harbour of Kuala Baram on the great Baram River where we embarked on one of the famous (or notorious, depending on your point of view) *Ekspres* boats - low slung, narrow like a big torpedo and capable of 60kph. This hurtles through the water, trying to avoid floating logs and other hazards which could - and sometimes do - capsize it. Tugs shove and pull great rafts of timber downstream. It is sad to see so much logging along the river because it makes you wonder whether the rainforest can survive for long at this rate. Fortunately a good deal is virtually inaccessible, even to determined loggers.

At the little town of Marudi we changed boats. Marudi is a pleasant place of small shops built round a market square. It was here that on James' suggestion we all bought tobacco to ward off the leeches we expected to be meeting, though we only half believed him when he said that tobacco down our socks would keep the little blighters at bay. On then to Long Terawan where we changed craft again to navigate the much smaller Melinau River which snaked away into the thick jungle. This time we climbed into a small motorised canoe or longboat which skimmed along with a man in the bows on the lookout for any hazards and

On the Headhunters' Trail, Borneo

to indicate by hand signals the best channels through the numerous shallows and rapids. It seems a point of honour among Sarawak boatmen to go as fast as possible under any circumstances.

At 6.30pm we pulled up at the jetty belonging to our lodge on the edge of the Mulu National Park. It had been a long, hot and at times exciting day of 11 hours.

For the next two days we explored the Mulu caves, the largest known to man and one of the world's great natural wonders. Underground rivers, fantastic formations and most remarkable of all, the spectacular evening flight of the bats - sixteen million of them - which come sweeping out of the Deer Cave. On the lip of the cave a bat hawk perched, waiting for supper. As he swooped to the kill you could just imagine the poor bat crying out 'Why me?' as he pondered the odds of 16 million to one. Inside the cave, wafts of ammonia assailed our nostrils from the piles of bat droppings everywhere - the locals call it 'black snow'.

We returned from the Deer Cave after dusk, when all the bats had gone. The way back to the river bank and our boat was across a mile or so of duckboards laid through the forest. A thunderstorm broke out, waking the jungle to screeching pandemonium, like something from a horror film, and when the rain stopped huge fireflies floated about through the dark trees like so many Tinkerbells. It was a magic walk, the like of which I have never experienced elsewhere.

Once we had explored the caves it was time to go deeper into the national park, so packing our belongings into a longboat we headed off up-river. The jungle closed in on both sides, but the river, though shallow, remained quite wide. The depth of water in the Melinau depends on the rainfall in the Mulu hills; it can rise or fall several feet in a few hours. Now it was low so here and there our little craft grounded on the gravel bottom and we had to jump out to float her off. Fortunately there are no crocodiles in the Melinau, but a long water snake rippled past, seemingly intent on reaching the bank.

We beached the boats at a place called Long Letut, which is just a clearing on the bank and seems no different from a dozen others except that this one has a track leading into the jungle. We followed the track warily at first - this was our first close encounter with the real thing. No duckboards to protect us here!

We followed the trail for a couple of hours or so until it eventually led us to a clearing in which we could see a rude shelter, very much like the huts in the *Tenko* TV programme - four walls, open at half height, and a tin roof. This was the celebrated Camp 5 and our home for the next couple of days. It was called Camp 5 because the explorers of this area established a number of camps, and this was the fifth. It marked the entrance to the Melinau Gorge and behind the hut the limestone cliffs rose sheer for 800ft . A large cave at the foot of the cliff was utilised as a cookhouse - limestone icicles hung down like menacing daggers at the cooks, though they didn't seem to mind.

The favourite excursion from Camp 5 is known as The Pinnacles, a steep scramble to some limestone pinnacles which rise arrow-like from the forest canopy. Despite the heavy rain some of our party attempted it next day and actually made the top though it took them eight hours of very strenuous effort. I turned back at half height, wet through and utterly exhausted.

The continuous rain caused the river to rise alarmingly and we became anxious because the next day we were due to tackle the most difficult part of the jungle, which involved several stream crossings. If the water was high we could be in for a tricky few hours. But by the time we crossed the rope bridge over the Melinau next morning the river level had fallen again and we were optimistic about our prospects. The jungle closed in and the path was difficult to follow - in fact it vanished. Without our two Iban tribesmen to show us the way we would have been utterly lost. Now and again we waded through streams shallow enough not to worry us, but there was one stream where we had to put our sacks on our heads and wade through a swift flowing current, waist deep.

Suddenly the jungle ended and we stood on the banks of a large river, the Terikan, where longboats awaited our arrival. Soon we were skimming down the river, avoiding rapids and rocks, until we came to the Medalam River and the longhouse at Rumah Jarom. Here we stayed, bivouacking on the verandah, whilst throughout the night heavily tattooed Iban hunters came and went on their search for game; usually wild pig. These longhouses are exactly as their name suggests - one long building, raised on stilts, and divided into numerous apartments, each housing a family. One apartment acted as the shop, selling simple necessities, not to mention beer and cigarettes. We ate with the chief; dried fish cooked in bamboo on a rice dish. Huge jars of rice wine stood around the dining area, but we were not offered any!

Next day we moved down-river to Limbang and civilisation - including one of the finest Chinese meals I have ever eaten. It was the end of our jungle trek and time to move on to Sabah and Mount Kinabalu.

5
Rivers and Lakes

S urprisingly, perhaps, there are very few adventure holidays based entirely on lakes. Probably the best in this direction are trips in Canada, using the Canadian style canoes. There are, of course, river tours which take in lakes along the way and I'll describe a particularly interesting one of these later. Rivers themselves are a different matter - there are interesting river tours in many parts of the world, some following the banks and others actually on the water. There is also the ultimate river experience - white water rafting!

The White Water Experience

W hite water rafting has in recent years become a feature of many adventure trips. It is undeniably exciting, and particularly since there are no fixed rules about it (despite what experts might tell you.) The white water referred to is caused by rapids where the smooth river breaks up into falls and chutes, often with standing waves or 'stoppers' which the raft tackles head on. The raft bucks, twists and jumps in an alarming fashion and at great speed. The water comes crashing aboard, and you think you are sure to die! When I rafted part of the Urubamba in Peru a few years ago a BBC reporter in the raft cried in horror when we rounded a bend and came face to face with a five foot wave, "Oh, my God! What have I let myself in for?!" Unfortunately, he was broadcasting at the time!

Jeff Rennicke, in his book *River Days*, one of the best books to convey the excitement of rafting, describes white water thus:

"... it is unlike anything else in the world of sports. Shooting rapids is a one-shot deal, the muzzleloader of water sports…whitewater requires that you get it right first time.

"First comes the roar of the water in the tight canyon, a sound like distant thunder, followed by the straining of the boatmen to see over the drop. The boat then seems to float out onto the tongue, a strangely quiet, slick spot where things go calm and smooth at the head of every rapid, like a lull before the storm - that first wave. Your heart pounds, your fists clench and you are in it: whitewater."

Rivers are graded in difficulty on an International Whitewater Rating System of I to VI. Grade I is gently moving water, Grade II entails waves up to 3ft with a clear channel, Grade III has waves up to 5ft with boulders and obstacles to navigate - and a roar, Grade IV is heavy water, with obstacles, huge waves and loud roar, Grade V requires skilled handling and is for the experts and Grade VI is unraftable; or at least too dangerous to try. Most commercial trips are III-IV, but a lot depends on the state of the river and on the local grading. I have rafted a Grade III river which was scarcely more than a stiff Grade II, and on the other hand I have rafted a Grade III which was every bit of Grade IV. Grade IV is as exciting as most folk would want.

No river is entirely made up of white water (though it may seem like it at times). There are long stretches of calmer water, where you can gather yourself together for the next onslaught. On some river trips (as distinct from pure white water trips) there may be relatively little in the way of white water, the purpose being to enjoy the river and its surroundings, maybe on a trip lasting days or even weeks. Doyen of the long trips (with plenty of rapids) is the Colorado which flows through the Grand Canyon in the USA. It was first travelled by John Wesley Powell and his team in wooden boats in 1869, when it was even fiercer than it is now because there were no dams in those days. It took him 100 days and is one of the great epics of exploration. Nowadays trips take up to three weeks. In 1965 only 547 people rafted through the canyon but in seven years this grew to 16,432! A strict permit system has restricted numbers since then. On some of the other American rivers, however, it is not unusual for there to be 100,000 rafters in a year.

Rafts and techniques vary. There are some huge rafts which carry entire encampments including the kitchen sink, and may even be motor powered, but most people experience the smaller raft, made of rubber, looking like an inshore lifeboat. Six or eight crewmen (boaters, the Americans call them) sit on the bulwarks, legs inside the raft, and armed with a paddle each attempts to follow the directions of the 'captain' who sits at the stern, steering. On some rafts there are 'oar trips' where all the work is done by the professional and you just sit back, doing nothing much. This is not as much fun, the experts say.

I have only experienced the paddle rafting. The raft may or may not be equipped with foot loops, which are very reassuring as you are less likely to tip into the river, but some rafters think they are dangerous if the raft flips over, because they may trap the person who has his foot stuck in a loop. Usually, on any rafting trip there's a bit of practice first so that the captain and crew understand what is wanted and what the commands mean. It is especially important to lean in the direction of river flow if the raft goes side on, because the water can get underneath and flip it. Kim Crumbo, river ranger for the Grand Canyon National Park, says there are only two kinds of boater - those who have flipped and those who are going to flip! Once you hit the rapids there is no time to think - instant reaction to the commands is required, but I am not at all convinced that the crew can control events!

All boatmen are equipped with lifejackets and should have helmets because of the rocks in the river. There are conflicting views on how to behave should you get flipped. You will be carried downstream rapidly and the thing to try and avoid is being bumped into rocks. One theory is to work yourself feet pointing downstream and go with the current, as that will carry you through the clear channels. Mmm.

Back in 1986 I narrowly missed a hair raising adventure on the River Beas in Kulu, India. It was a meeting of the Indian Mountaineering Foundation and they had arranged for a couple of rafts on the Beas. There weren't enough places for everyone but I was lucky enough to win one, only to have to give it up when I damaged my hand and could not hold a paddle. Doug Scott took my place. But something went sadly wrong. Instead of the Grade III they were expecting they were soon in Grade IV/V, the rafts flipped and there was a desperate struggle to get ashore, helped by watching locals. Nobody seems to know what happened to the rafts! According to Doug it was a very hairy experience - and he's a connoisseur in such things!

A few years later on the Stanislaus River of California my own turn came. This is a III/IV river with several named falls, of which the most notorious is Big Dog. We pulled out of the river to make an inspection of Big Dog from the bank - a usual tactic for serious falls, so that the captain can work out which line to take when it comes to the crunch. It looked horrendous, like a miniature version of Niagara. But we got in the raft, felt the tremendous pull of the current and then in a stupendous crash surged over the fall in a welter of spray and adrenalin. We were through! Whether in relief or elation the skipper turned the boat side on without warning us. Caught unawares we had no time to adjust our balance. The current swept under the raft and we flipped. I was suddenly aware of being under the water, and I thought how remarkably clear it looked. Then I bobbed up like a cork and found myself being swept downriver towards the next falls, called the Widdowmaker. Fortunately I was able, eventually, to reach the bank where willing hands hauled me ashore. We all survived, I am glad to say, and recovering the raft, continued downstream without further incident.

A couple of points were brought home by this incident. First, there should always be more than one raft in a party, so that help is at hand. Second, it is foolish to carry valuables like cameras on a trip (none of us was) and lastly, if like me you wear glasses, make sure they have a retaining cord!

America leads the world in river rafting. Apart from the Grand Canyon (and other canyon runs) of the Colorado River, there are the American, Klamath, Tuolumne and Stanislaus rivers of California, the Deschutes, Rogue and Owyhee rivers of Oregon, the Salmon, Snake and Selway rivers of Idaho, the Gunnison Gorge of Colorado, the Tatshenshini of Alaska, and many more. Worldwide there are famous runs on the Urubamba in Peru, the Zambesi in Africa, the Sun Kosi of Nepal, the Beas of India, Landsborough of New

Rafting instruction of the Mohaka River, New Zealand
(photo: New Zealand Tourist Board)

Zealand, the Omo of Ethiopia and the Inn of Austria. To name but a few!

You can always opt out of the day's rafting on a general trip but if you are not sure whether you will like it, it is possible to have a trial run at home with the National Whitewater Centre in Wales (01678 521083) and Splash in Scotland (01887 829706) or in England try Nottingham for artificial whitewater runs (01159 813222). No British rivers come anywhere near the overseas ones however.

There are two esoteric variations on rafting which I came across in New Zealand's South Island, the home of every type of adventure. One is river surfing, where instead of using a raft you surf board down a white water river, the Kawarau, near Queenstown. Naturally, you lie on the board, not stand on it, and it is called by its originators 'serious fun' - I bet it is. The other is at Greytown, on the West Coast and is - would you believe - cave rafting. This is white water rafting but done underground! They use the Taniwha Cave series, and there is a gentler option of just floating through the caves in a large guided raft. The place is alive with glow-worms, which form a spectacular backdrop to the adventure. If you have never seen massed glow-worms, you have a treat in store - well worth a diversion to see some if you get the opportunity.

We might as well mention here another water activity which is sometimes offered to adventure travellers, and that is jet-boating, another New Zealand invention. These craft, large speedboats powered by water jets, are capable of skimming at high speed over shallow rivers where ordinary propeller boats can't go. They seat half a dozen people or so and are driven by a skilled jet-boater who can do heart-stopping manoeuvres like spinning the craft on a sixpence, and just avoiding head on collisions with rocks. I have jet-boated the Shotover River at Queenstown and very exciting it was, too, but not as 'hairy' as a tough white water ride. You quickly get blasé over a jet-boat ride, which is something you never do with white water!

Bambi-burgers and Gold: Paddling the Oulanka, Finland

I f there is anywhere in the world where water predominates it has to be Finland. Half the country seems to be lakes and rivers, and they claim to have more lakes than anyone else - a claim hotly disputed by neighbouring Sweden, incidentally. There is some white water - the River Kitka, for example - but there is also plenty of opportunity for touring by Canadian canoe.

One region for exploring is the Oulanka National Park up in the far north near the town of Kuusamo. There's a four or five day trek through the *taiga* here called the Bears' Ring, which touches several lakes and the Kitka and Oulanka rivers. The *taiga* is the name for the wetlands forest, with pools and swamps. It is home to wolves, wolverines and bears though you are unlikely to see any from the path, and straying from the path in all that bog is not recommended. You are much more likely to see reindeer in the drier parts. There are huts and campsites, but as with all these northern wastelands, the midges or mosquitoes are a problem.

A group of us, led by the genial giant Jokke Kämäräinen, who runs Ruka Safaris, took our canoes out onto the Oulanka River. We launched in a quiet pool just below the impressive Kiutagongas Falls, which came roaring down a gorge and dissipated their energy into the broad waters of the pool, surprisingly with scarce a ripple. It didn't take us long to get the hang of the two-man canoes - just a question of each knowing what the other is going to do.

We paddled off down the broad river into a veritable wilderness. An impenetrable forest of tall pines rose on either hand. The silence was profound, disturbed only by the ripple of the paddles.

There were shallows where we had to navigate carefully, choosing one out of several alternative channels, hoping it wasn't a dead-end. Here and there reindeer stood on the bank, little groups with their foals. At lunchtime we pulled out onto a gravel beach, lit a wood fire and cooked our lunch which was reindeer steaks (we called them bambi-burgers, I'm sorry to say.). Whilst waiting for the water to boil for coffee Jokke picked up a handful of gravel and carefully washing it in his huge palm showed us the tiny shimmering flecks remaining among the pebbles. Gold! Well, I've been caught like that before and claimed it was pyrites - fool's gold - but no, it really was gold. The river is full of the stuff, but it will never be exploited because the whole area is a national park and, in any case, the extraction would probably cost more than the gold is worth.

After lunch we paddled down the river until at last we could go no further. It wasn't that the river had run out but stern warnings appeared on the bank announcing the Russian border. Jokke had arranged for us to be picked up by truck and transported to our base. Later we went to a camp by Lake Kitka where in the big tent we lay like Romans on reindeer skins whilst we ate a feast

The source of the River Lison in the French Jura, one of the most spectacular river heads in Europe

of wild mushrooms, salmon and cloudberries with cream. Then into the next tent which, incredibly, was rigged up as a sauna. Sauna is practically a religion in Finland, but a portable sauna was something new. It is taken in the nude of course and we cooled off by skinny dipping in the lake.

Across the Peneda Hills to the Rio Lima, Portugal

Following the course of a river on foot can have its rewards, usually of the gentler kind. A number of the French GR paths follow rivers, and I remember a walk along the rivers Loue and Lison in the Jura, which culminated at the spectacular head of the Lison where the water pours out of a cave in the limestone like a Niagara. There are some pretty French villages on the way and lots of forest paths.

This walk was organised by Headwater, using the system which has become popular in the last few years, whereby heavy luggage is taken by vehicle from one hotel to the next, allowing you to enjoy the walk unencumbered with anything more than a day sack. Sometimes there is a guide to lead the party, but on the Loue-Lison walk a couple of us were literally left to our own

Washing clothes on the Rio Lima, Portugal

devices, armed only with a map and route card. This is not too difficult where the paths are well defined, and more exciting perhaps, though I can think of some places where it could be tricky. We had a guide with us for a walk in Portugal which combined hill-walking and a river and was organised by Alternative Travel.

The Penedes-Gerês National Park is a remote area, scarcely known in Britain. It is not unlike parts of Scotland. Our aim was to cross the hills from Porto Rivero in the north to Soajo in the south, then follow the Rio Lima downstream to Ponte de Lima.

The hills rise to some 4,500ft, sometimes as craggy ridges, sometimes as rounded domes covered by scrub. They are home to deer, wild boar and even wolves and though we saw none of these, we did see a small group of wild Luso-Galician ponies, which seemed quite unconcerned at our approach. Delicate rock-rose and tall asphodel grew alongside tumbling banks of heavenly blue lithospermum and here and there tiny miniature narcissus could be found - the advantage of a spring tour. Another advantage was the fine weather, which was never so hot as to make tackling the steep slopes arduous.

Our first day took us over the ridges, past a large pool, set among smooth granite boulders reminiscent of Arran, where the croaking of thousands of frogs was deafening. A frogs' chorus is common enough in rivers and jungles throughout the world, but this was the daddy of them all - it sounded like a hundred brass bands warming up for a championship. Beyond the pool a very steep descent took us to the hamlet of Senhora da Peneda. We could look down on the hamlet in an almost aerial view - a little Toytown beneath our boots. Here there is a huge church set in an elegant plaza, which was once a place of pilgrimage. Far too grand for this remote valley (only recently connected to the outside world by a proper road) it would have been more at home in Madrid. But a shepherd once had a vision of the Virgin on this spot and hence the shrine, though sceptics say the real reason was to attract some of the lucrative pilgrim trade that passed nearby on the way to Santiago de Compostella.

Be that as it may, the locals point out with pride that they have proof that the shrine protects them. About 50 years ago a huge piece of rock weighing many tons broke off from the great crag which overhangs the village. Death and destruction seemed inevitable, and yet a miracle happened. The rock bounced clear over the church, hit the plaza, then bounced over the houses into the river without touching a thing.

Next day we walked down the Peneda Valley and over the hills to Soajo (pronounced 'swaaj'). Tiny hamlets clustered in forgotten corries where roads were a new invention. Previously the inhabitants had to make do with bridle paths paved with slabs of the local granite and just wide enough to take a small ox-cart. The carts were still there, trundling their way in ruts worn centimetres deep over the centuries.

Even the smaller paths were often paved and a delight to walk on. Sometimes, though, we left the paths entirely to take to the open hillside or fields (in Portugal they have a sensible 'right to roam anywhere' policy) and struggled with boulder-strewn slopes or jumped babbling streams, but before long another paved path would appear to ease our way. Only near the villages did we meet other people and throughout the entire tour we did not come across another tourist walking these hills.

We walked out of the hills to the valley of the Rio Vez at Arcos de Valdevez, where we stayed at an old manor house. The walking was henceforth along the banks of the Rio Vez and Rio Lima. The barren uplands gave way to lush pastures and woods with the wide, swiftly flowing rivers always to hand. Vines trailed across pergolas and wild yellow lupins sprouted from the riverbanks. In the rich fields maize and beans were grown together; the beans putting back in the soil the nourishment the maize was taking out.

When the Roman army reached the River Lima, they thought it was the River Lethe, the river of forgetfulness in Greek mythology, and their commander was forced to wade across first and call each man over by name, to show his memory was not impaired!

Our walk took us by quiet waters to Ponte de Lima, past women still using the river to do the family washing, past fishermen and ancient derelict water mills, and past the Romanesque church of São Salvador at Bravaes with its beautiful doorway. It was a long day, but the last walk of the tour. Next day we drove down to Oporto and, crossing the River Duoro to Vila Nova de Gaia, spent the afternoon sampling the wine lodges.

Kashmir With a Difference

There was once a Moghul Emperor, so the story goes, who as he lay dying was asked if there was anything he wished for. "Only Kashmir", he said, and expired. Anyone who has visited that lovely land will know what he meant and will know why the Moghuls built some of their finest pleasure gardens there. How tragic that at present this beautiful country is torn by religious strife and no longer safe for travellers. Let us hope that some day peace will return. The heartland of the country is the Vale of Kashmir, with lakes and canals, and the River Jhelum, on whose banks lies Srinagar, the capital.

Because it is in the mountains, Kashmir has an equable summer climate, making it an ideal place to escape the heat of the plains. This is what the Moghuls did and so did the British when they ruled India. The problem for the British, however, was that they did not rule Kashmir itself - that was an independent 'native state', whose ruler was canny enough to pass a law forbidding foreigners (ie. the British) from owning land or building houses. The British in turn, being equally canny, responded by building boats - houseboats. And thus the tradition of the Kashmir houseboats began and continues to this day.

Today's houseboats are much bigger than their predecessors. Each has four or five bedrooms with en suite bathrooms, a kitchen, a dining room, a lounge and a verandah. Every boat has an exotic name, often faintly ludicrous, such as *Hollywood* or *New Moon* painted on a large board over the verandah. Built of deodar wood and ornately carved, they cost a small fortune to build and can last 80 years. On the Dal Lake, next to Srinagar, there are dozens of them.

Plying from houseboat to houseboat and to and from the shore are small punts called *shikara*, a name which also applies to the boatman himself. They bring every conceivable sort of goods and services for sale, from a box of matches to a massage; a ten rupee trinket to a sapphire necklace the price of which would make you blink.

The penalty for all this is that you can't go for a stroll: you have to be paddled ashore by a shikara. There's usually one attached to the boat awaiting your pleasure, but you tend not to bother except for planned excursions into town or the Moghul gardens. In a houseboat life tends to come to you rather than the other way round.

You can get very lazy, cossetted like this, especially if you don't feel like trekking into the mountains, but one day some friends and I, from Exodus, hit upon the idea of using shikaras to explore the rivers and canals. In particular we decided to try to reach Lake Wular, about 30km to the north and claimed to be the largest freshwater lake in Asia, about 160km^2. Historical records showed that there was an island in the lake known simply as Lanka, which means island, and that the Moghul Emperor Akbar had a summer palace there in the 16th century. Why not see what the old boy was up to?

Nobody we knew had ever done this trip, but by a strange coincidence some years later I found it described (though in the opposite direction) in a pre-war *Murray's Handbook to India* picked up in a second-hand bookshop in Cape Town. The ruin on Lanka was described as a temple.

Six travellers and twelve staff crammed into two shikaras together with all the cooking and camping gear, and set off across the Dal Lake. There is a dream-like quality about floating on the Dal Lake; the placid water scarcely rippling along the thwarts, white bridges crossing little canals, distant minarets and the green hills over all. We lay in cushioned splendour whilst the boys paddled lazily along. This was certainly trekking with a difference!

From Dal Lake we floated gently into Nagin Lake, once regarded as the place for up-market houseboats. If you could afford to live on the Nagin Lake you were *somebody*, in the days of the Raj! It is smaller than Dal Lake with its tree lined banks fringing admirably clear water for bathing but it lacks the bustle and life which is such a feature of the houseboats on the larger lake.

From the Nagin Lake we entered a series of canals, the Nulla Amirkhan, which took us around Srinagar, slowly circling the great Moghul fort on its hilltop. Sometimes these canals were so narrow we seemed to be floating in a tree lined tunnel; sometimes so shallow than we grounded and had to be rescued by the boys jumping overboard and pushing us free. From time to time we passed a poverty-stricken hut perched precariously on the canal bank and at one place came to a clear stretch where the *dhobie wallahs* were doing laundry in the age-old way of beating hell out of the clothes on a stone. The water of the canal was a muddy brown, and I hate to think what was in it, yet the laundry hung on the lines drying was white as driven snow. How do they do it?

At last we broke free from the canals and came to Anchar Lake, once a bird sanctuary but now largely left to its fate. It is rarely visited by travellers. The water is covered in reeds for the most part but the birds are still in evidence - two varieties of kingfisher, the golden oriel and the occasional fish eagle. Shikaras laden with cut reeds floated past us and there was scarcely a time when the water was not busy with traffic; shikaras carrying reeds, lotus plants, even gravel. Some of the gravel boats had a freeboard of barely an inch and seemed likely to sink at any moment. There was more traffic in a day on the Anchar Lake than I'd seen in a month on the Manchester Ship Canal.

The navigation of the complex canals and lakes was something to wonder at, for it was like following a water maze. Sometimes our crew would ignore a seemingly obvious opening and head for a barely distinguishable break in the reeds, but they were always right, of course. I decided that there was no way anyone could navigate round the Vale of Kashmir without a local guide.

When eventually we joined the Jhelum River we were jolted out of our complacency. Here was no placid lake, no limpid canal - the Jhelum was a wide, stoutly flowing river that caught the boats and whisked them along like corks in a gutter. Once our nerves had settled the sensation was fine and the crew loved it because they didn't need to paddle. But for all the good things of life there is usually payment to be made. We suddenly found we were travelling upstream, against the current, and this was a yashmak of a different hue! We had to get out and pull the boats with ropes, like Chinese trackers on the Yangtze River. I'm not sure how we came to change direction; perhaps we changed rivers and were following the Sind. Without a map it was hard to tell.

When we stopped for lunch the meal was cooked aboard one of the boats, whilst we lounged in the shade of a chenar tree, but in the evening we set up an idyllic camp on the river bank watched by a group of beautiful and wide-eyed Kashmiri girls. We cooked on a wood fire in the camp, the blue smoke curling up into the clear evening air, the river gliding silently by.

Next day we sailed into the lovely Manasbal Lake; a tiny jewel set among the hills. The water was crystal clear and we dived in. Manasbal reminded me strongly of Grasmere in the English Lake District, but the sense is illusory for Manasbal is 4km long and a kilometre wide and the hills rise to 2000m round about it - a much grander scale all round than Grasmere.

About lunchtime we entered a small canal which led into the Wular Lake. On the skyline, high and white, rose Haramukh (5148m). The light shimmered off the distant parts of the lake, like a mirage, and at first I couldn't believe my eyes for it seemed as though a man was driving cattle across the water. But it was no illusion; Wular may be the biggest lake, but it is also the shallowest. Even its size - 20km long and 8km wide - varies from season to season and another surprising thing is that despite being shallow it can be subject to the most violent storms. Where we entered the lake the surface was covered with water chestnuts and it was hard work paddling the boats through them towards Lanka, a little island covered in trees.

Eventually we scrambled ashore, smug in the knowledge that we had made our goal. From the island's undergrowth ancient stones poked out. Was this the scant remains of a temple or the last vestiges of some royal pleasure dome? It wasn't possible to tell, but I suspect the latter. The undergrowth looked vaguely familiar, and then it dawned on us - no wonder old Akbar was

On the canal at Srinagar, Kashmir. Even in more settled times, this journey by canals and rivers to Lake Wular was seldom done

fond of Lanka, for the whole place was one vast hashish nursery!

The crew gathered bundles of the stuff and that night we had an unusual *omelette aux fines herbes*. I can't say that it tasted any different, but I certainly slept soundly.

6
Islands

Islands have always had a special place in our affections, perhaps because we are an island race or perhaps because we remember *Treasure Island* from our childhood. Holiday islands never lack for customers; Madeira, Majorca and the islands of the Caribbean vie with one another in their beaches, and the luxury of their hotels. Not, you might think, the place for adventure and yet there is adventure enough in some of these places - diving in the Blue Grottoes of the Caribbean, for example, or walking the wild hills of Majorca.

There are so many islands. Instinctively we think of palm-fringed lagoons and coral strands but there are others cold enough to bring memories of brass monkeys, such as Baffin Island, to the far north of Canada, with its stark granite peaks sticking up like huge slabs of cake turned on end, or Spitzbergen, the bleak arctic home of polar bears. Adventure enough in those - and there are travel companies which will take you there, if that's what you want.

It depends what you mean by an island, of course. Australia is an island, but not for our purposes. Similarly Borneo's chief characteristics have nothing to do with being an island. I think the island should be fairly small and the sea should never be too far away. Walking and sailing are the adventures here.

Corsica's Rugged Mountains

Corsica is both a mountain and island paradise. There's plenty of sun, sea and sand on this Mediterranean jewel, with a rugged coastline and unspoilt villages and a bonus in the shape of pink granite mountains running the length of the island. Walking and climbing are both popular activities. North of the capital, Ajaccio, there is excellent walking which starts in the village of Ota and goes via the Spelunca Gorge to Evisa and the foothills of Monte Cinto (2710m), the highest peak in the island. This can be continued on to Corte, the ancient capital of Corsica, taking four or five days in all. It is part of the much longer Mare à Mare Nord route.

Evisa is a good centre where there are plenty of walks. Near at hand is the Aitone Forest laced with several tracks through the Corsican pines, where the woods are never too dense to obscure the view down the Porto Valley to the pink granite spires of the Tre Signore. On the coast the headland of Capu Rossu with its ancient tower set on red rocks is another worthwhile trip, the path winding through banks of potentilla, cistus and bergamot and giving superb views out over an azure blue sea. This can be combined with a walk on the

Walking on the Calanches peaks of the Corsican coast.
The island offers a variety of walking

crags of the Calanche where good tracks lead up through fantastic rock spires with amazing ease in situations you might have thought imposs- ible.'A forest of purple granite' Guy de Maupassant called it. Another walk re- membered for its flowers is to the Lago de Creno, where in early summer the mountain path is bordered by banks of hellebores, and where, just beyond the little lake, there is one of the most dramatic mountain views you could imagine, with the land falling away into a deep valley of tumbled rocks, trees and waterfalls, like a Japanese print.

But the real gem of Corsica is the traverse of the mountains known as the Corsican High Level Route, the GR20. It is claimed to be the toughest of all the French Grande Randonnées and suitable only for the experienced mountain walker. It is regarded as one of the great walks of the world. It stretches from Calenzana in the north to Conca in the south, 178km, and takes about a fortnight. There are campsites and mountain huts en route. It can be done in either direction, of course, but for those who cannot afford to do the entire walk there is a shorter version which just takes in the northern half, known as the Haute Corse, which takes eight days and stretches 90km. This is usually done from south to north, and is the tougher half of the route, with 6300m of ascent and descent.

The GR20 crosses some fine mountain ridges, strong granite peaks with towering walls of rock all round. The crux is the Cirque de la Solitude, surrounded by the peaks of Punta Minuta, Bocca Minuta and Pic von Cube. The descent to the cirque involves steep but not technically demanding scrambling with some fixed chains and ladders.

Despite their position in the Mediterranean, Corsican mountains carry snow for much of the year - often from late October to June - and the GR20 would be very tough under those conditions, calling for mountaineering experience and equipment. The walk is most popular in July and August, because of school holidays, but it is actually very hot during these months and if you have the choice, September would be better. Not only would the walking be pleasanter, but there would be more room in the huts.

The huts can be a problem with overcrowding, and backpacking, camping near the huts or on the campsites might be preferred, but of course that means carrying all the necessary gear on what is already a tough route. Water supplies can be unreliable so it is necessary to carry plenty of water, especially in summer, and at least six days' food.

J ust as in some areas dogs can be a nuisance, in Corsica it is pigs. One of the favourite dishes on the island's menus is wild boar, but I suspect much of it is wild pig. The pigs roam around in thuggish gangs, bringing back strong memories of *Animal Farm*. They almost certainly belong to someone, but it never seems like it. Occasionally they block the highway and anyone driving on the island's narrow twisting roads needs to keep a sharp lookout, or it won't be just the brakes squealing! Some of the island campsites are like prison compounds, not to stop the campers getting out, but to stop the pigs getting in!

Dogs can be dealt with - a trekking pole will generally fend them off if necessary and there is even a sonic gadget called a 'Fazer' which is supposed to make any dog retreat. I wonder if a 'Fazer' works on pigs?

Majorcan Hills

M ajorca is usually thought of as a package holiday mecca with sun, sex and sangria in equal proportions, but away from the popular beaches it is another Mediterranean island which offers adventurous walking, though not on the grand scale of Corsica. The whole northern side of the island, especially the north-east around Pollensa, is very mountainous and has some very fine walks. These tend to be day walks, done with the aid of a hire car, though there is a well-known continuous trek from Valldemossa to Pollensa of three or four days which is unusual in including a night in a monastery! And unless you are a particularly strong walker you'll probably end up doing a mountain bivvy as well. It is a superbly wild walk and no doubt similar routes could be devised elsewhere in these remote hills.

Even more than in Corsica, the summer months are too hot for walking. Spring and autumn are the walking months here - though even mid-winter can be good. There is frequently snow, but this is not as serious as in Corsica, or as deep. The hotels of Pollensa are now alive to the walkers' interests - in fact they presented June Parker, the author of the definitive guide to walking on the island, with a plaque and celebratory dinner for the way she had extended the tourist season! Pollensa, Soller or Cala san Vicente are the best centres. Hotels and apartments tend to be cheap in the off-season months (the in-season for walkers.) and cheap package flights are still available. Walking the Majorcan hills is probably the most affordable of all adventure holidays.

My first experience of Majorcan hill-walking took place one July, which was entirely the wrong time of the year. I knew this but reckoned that if I chose an 'easy' route, it would be alright. So from the new Parker guide as it then was I chose a ridge called La Coma (now called La Serra de la Punta). I started soon after seven a.m. and thought I was in for a simple stroll but it turned out to be anything but. Before long the fierce heat of the sun beat down like a furnace and the ridge proved to be rocky, tricky and covered with the prickly scrub *Smilax balearica,* which plucked at my clothes abominably. It was worse than the wait-a-bit shrubs of the African bush - and a warning not to wear shorts. From time to time I was able to escape onto a rock outcrop but progress was slow and by the time I reached the summit, at the end of the long ridge, I felt a dehydrated wreck. The descent to Puerto Pollensa was a nightmare and I reached the town on the verge of collapse. Some years later I happened to climb La Coma again, in the proper season, but by a shorter and nicer route and whilst I was on the top I saw someone approaching along the ridge. He proved to be English and as he dropped exhausted at my feet he gasped, "I've done this damned ridge four times now, and it still knackers me!" It is not often one meets a practising masochist. By this time Parker had revised the grade of the ridge sharply upwards!

Majorca is an excellent choice if you are not sure that adventure is for you. There are any number of easy walks like the Boquer Valley beloved by bird-watchers, or the Puig de Maria, a small hill above Pollensa, and you are never far from civilization.

There are also some arduous trips to be had like the Pareis Gorge (see Ch 7) or the Cavall Bernat ridge whose pinnacled crest is like a giant coxcomb over the Boquer Valley - on the opposite side it plummets over a thousand feet sheer into the ocean. But there is plenty in between the extremes. Many walks are on the sort of paths we would call bridleways, often restored by ICONA (El Instituto Nacional para la Conservacion de la Natureleza), the national institute for nature conservation. ICONA also erects small shelters here and there, but there are no mountain refuges on the island at which one can stay

*On the Atalaya de Alcudia in Majorca -
a splendid introduction to island walking*

as there are in Corsica. All the walks can be done in a day, to and from a parked car - a hired car is absolutely necessary in Majorca.

A short but interesting excursion is that to the Peña Roja, a black rocky tooth on the Alcudia peninsula. The climb begins at the Ermita de la Victoria, a great bulk of a building, and follows a wide track which eventually traverses a steep hillside then narrows and climbs up through an arch in the rock. There are fixed chains for protection and a hopeful wooden handrail which looks as though it would collapse at the merest touch. The path is narrow, exposed, though not difficult and it leads to an old stone hut.

I climbed up to the hut one spring day to discover that the crux of the adventure lay above me - the final rock tooth. A steep scramble took me up to a gap in a narrow ridge, on the edge of all things, where the rock was only inches wide and from where an airy scramble led to the top of the final pinnacle. And guess what? On the very summit there was a cannon! A real 18th-century cannon of the sort that Nelson used. How the hell did they get it there in an age when there were no helicopters to lift things?

You can see why the cannon might be needed. It commanded the entrance to Pollensa Bay. But what a rotten place to do your National Service - imagine being told to nip down and get the ammo!

Because the Peña takes only a couple of hours to climb it is easy to combine it with the Atalaya de Alcudia but the Atalaya is much better climbed by the Fontanelles route which encapsulates all that is best in the easier Majorcan walking adventures.

One day a friend and I climbed through scented pinewoods to the open plateau below the mountain. The track was uncertain, not easy to follow at this stage, but by keeping more or less parallel to the ridge above us we eventually came to Fontanelles Valley which cut a deep V into the hills. A small stream trickled down the valley and there was a path of sorts, heavily obscured by shrubs and tall grasses. Up above there was a distinct gap in the ridge known as the Coll de ses Fontanelles (Coll is Majorquin for col) which proved tough going to reach and even tougher to descend the other side. The surroundings were wild. The path virtually disappeared and it became a question of reading the land, interpreting the ridges and delphs. It was all there, but it needed determination to sort it out.

Just when we were starting to have doubts we struck a broad bridleway that leads through the woods to another col, the Coll Baix. Here ICONA had built a shelter and there is a narrow path down to the shore at the Playa Baix, a long way below. We watched a tiny steamer plough a white furrow through the azure blue sea, then turned towards the bulk of the Atalaya which rose on our left. It looked steep and formidable but in fact ICONA had built a superb path which zig-zagged up the slopes. The views down to the beach and out to sea were incredible.

It ended in a minor scramble, as many of these Majorcan peaks do, and from the summit the views ranged over Pollensa and Alcudia bays. The way down couldn't have been simpler - the tourist path descended in a sweeping curve to the Ermitage, and then a narrow path by a babbling brook led to the road and the car.

For anyone with some experience of hillwalking in Britain, Majorca makes a next logical step to expanding their horizons, without having to learn the complexities of snow and ice as you do in the Alps, or problems with altitude. Another point in its favour is that it requires no extra gear to what you would wear in the UK.

Darwin's Paradise - Sailing Round the Galapagos Islands

About a thousand kilometres off the coast of Ecuador in South America lies a group of volcanic islands called the Galapagos. Formerly they were known as the Encantadas, or Enchanted Isles. Once the calling place for whalers and pirates, these lonely islands were visited by Charles Darwin during the memorable voyage of the *Beagle* in 1835. Recognizing how unique was the flora and fauna he commented specially on the Galapagos finches, of

A saddleback tortoise at the Charles Darwin Research Station at Puerta Ayora in the Galapagos. Experts can even tell which part of an island a tortoise comes from

which there are 13 separate species - all finches, but all different. Also the fact that the giant tortoises, for which the islands are famous, should be different from island to island struck him as odd. (Some experts reckon they can tell not only which island but which *part* of an island a tortoise comes from.) What Darwin saw on the Galapagos was instrumental in developing his theory of the Origin of Species.

There are 13 major islands, 6 minor islands and 42 named islets in the archipelago, along with scores of unnamed rocks. All are volcanic in origin and some are still active from time to time; volcanic cones and vast lava flows are features which dominate much of the landscape. They look like bits dropped off the moon. Only four of the islands are inhabited: Floreana, Isabela, San Cristóbal, and Santa Cruz. The capital is Puerto Baquerizo Moreno on San Cristóbal Island with about 2500 souls, or rather less than half the total population. There's a landing strip here and on Baltra Island, with flights to Guayaquil in Ecuador, the country which owns the islands. Owing to the popularity of the Galapagos, resources, especially water, are very stretched and there is always talk of restricting tourist numbers, though because of the income tourism brings it is a difficult decision for a poor country to make. Visitors pay a hefty tax on landing.

It is the wide variety of amazing wildlife which is the chief attraction of the Galapagos - 875 different plants, 56 birds, 24 reptiles and 6 mammals, none of which shows the slightest fear of humans. The comical looking blue-footed boobies not only don't fly off as you approach but actually lay their eggs in the middle of the paths in open defiance. It is an animal idyll - or would be but for the wild predators introduced by Man in past centuries. These feral animals - pigs, goats, rats and what have you - attack anything that's going. Their effect on the tortoise population has been devastating. There is an intermittent but ineffectual control programme.

To help preserve the tortoises and to research the wildlife in general there is the Charles Darwin Research Station at Puerto Ayora on Santa Cruz, funded partly by the government and partly by world-wide conservation bodies. As with most research projects, it tends to be underfunded. The islands were declared a National Park in 1959.

I suppose the ultimate way to explore the Galapagos would be to fly into Baltra, hire a boat and spend weeks sailing from island to island. Even if the authorities permitted you to land (and they won't) you still wouldn't see them all - the two northern islands of Darwin and Wolf (or Culpepper and Wenman - all the islands have dual identities) are virtually inaccessible with cliffs rising sheer for 200m out of the ocean. Nobody stood on Culpepper until a helicopter landed there is 1964! And on Wenman, though there are beaches, few have scaled the cliffs beyond leading to the interior. On Pinta Island there is a line of cliffs 400m high, described as "awesome".

It is possible to cruise the islands in luxury but more fun to do as my group did and go on one of the small motor yachts, where a dozen of us crammed into the tiny cabins and the menu every day consisted of whatever fish we could catch. It was a mixed bag of hard-bitten journalists, a radio reporter from BBC's Breakaway travel programme and Bill Oddie, who was then President of the RSPB, on the lookout for birds, all led by Rocio Nicolalde, a beautiful local guide. The good ship *Xavier*, hired by Exodus Travels for the trip, was fairly primitive but we all got along fine.

The one thing you soon learn about the Pacific is that it can belie its name. The weather was hot but the seas were rough as we battered our way from island to island over the next few days, the boat a bucking bronco. That first night we were glad to drop anchor next to Pinnacle Rock, which rose like a huge spear from the waters in the lovely bay of Bartolomé Island. The bay sheltered us so we had a calm night and next day sailed across the short channel to Santiago Island, where a vast sheet of black lava lay petrified into the ripples and surges that had formed centuries ago when it flowed as an incandescent stream to the sea. It was pure moonscape; a dead world. And yet it wasn't truly dead. There were Sally Lightfoot crabs scuttling about, the ubiquitous sea lions, lava lizards and iguanas.

Returning to St Bartolomé we climbed up to the top of an old volcanic cone where we surprised a Galapagos hawk, a rare bird these days. It eyed us with disdain then flapped away slowly. On Pinnacle Rock penguins gamboled. The water was so calm and blue that we gave up birdwatching and went for a swim.

Next day we made a choppy crossing of five hours to South Plaza Island; a flat island of scrub and *Opuntia,* a tree cactus, beneath which grow patches of the bright red succulent *Sesuvivum.* This is the place to see land iguanas, scarcer than the marine variety; brown and four feet long, living dragons, but quite harmless. Access on Plaza is strictly controlled; the paths are marked out and it is forbidden to step off them. Down on the shore the bull sea lions were disputing the landing stage with the visitors. You don't argue with a 9ft, ton and a half of sea lion, so it took some time to get away!

At dawn we sailed to Puerto Ayora on Santa Cruz, a very rough crossing indeed which many of us spent hanging over the ship's side. But Peurto Ayora proved to be a delightful little town where they were actually boatbuilding on the shore; the timber ribs rising like the skeleton of a whale, adzed and sawn by muscle power alone. A little way inland we came to the Charles Darwin Research Centre where Sylvia Harcourt, the assistant to the Director, took us round showing us the giant tortoises and telling us about her work. Later, at the Sol y Mar bar I sipped a beer, sharing a concrete terrace with a dozen splendid black marine iguanas. They kept so still that at first I thought they were models put there as a tourist gimmick, until one of them, finding my company boring, flipped off the terrace into the sea.

In the late afternoon we sailed through calm waters for once to little Santa Fe Island and fetched up in a delightful bay where we all went swimming with the sea lions. The females (seven times smaller than the males) love to play and are delighted when you swim with them.

Next day the little *Xavier* passed through the split in the huge Kicker Rock. Two blades of basalt rise 150m from the sea leaving a narrow passage between. I found it an eerie journey. It seemed as though the rocks were about to turn in and crush the boat for being so presumptuous. It is home to many frigatebirds who have the alarming habit of puffing out huge bright red balloons beneath their bills.

By now the weather had turned very hot and the sea perfectly calm, a marvellous clear green-blue. We pulled into a tiny bay at Lobos Island for another swim. I dived in and swam above the crystal sands. Suddenly the sand moved and an enormous manta ray, with a flick of its powerful tail, shot away beneath me. These rays can reach 20ft across the body, but this one was smaller than that, though enough to make me head for my towel pretty quick!

Our wanderings had brought us near to San Cristóbal Island by this time so we sailed for Puerto Baquerizo Moreno, which lies on the west coast of that island. It is a pretty little place though it didn't seem as prosperous as Puerto Ayora. The hills above the town were shrouded in mist but we all piled into a truck and were driven up a long rough track towards them. The vegetation changed as we bumped and bounced our way up to the ramshackle village of Progreso, once a prison colony and now depending for a living on bananas, oranges and wild guavas. Above the village the countryside became almost like a Scottish moor and we abandoned the truck and walked up to a crater where we discovered a large green lake, partly obscured by the drifting mists. It could have been a lochan in the Cairngorms. The only freshwater streams in the Galapagos flow from this lake.

This ended our exploration of the Galapagos. It is a place to see wildlife such as you will not see elsewhere and where Nature does not fear Man. It is not a place to go walking; access is forbidden on many of the islands, strictly controlled on others and virtually impossible on some because of the ankle twisting lava flows and thorn bushes. But it's a grand sea-going adventure; island hopping in the best Pacific traditions. Just pray for calm weather!

The Islands of Atlantis

Far out into the Atlantic, almost a thousand miles from anywhere, lie the nine islands of the Azores, Europe's furthest west. It is tempting to think of them as remnants of the lost Atlantis, though when the Portuguese first discovered them in 1427 they had no traces of previous habitation. But they are volcanic, rising sheer out of an ocean $2^{1/2}$ miles deep - so who is to say that the cataclysm which destroyed the legendary Atlantis didn't throw up the Azores at the same time?

The archipelago has three groups of islands strung out across the ocean for a considerable distance. In the middle are five islands: Pico, Fayal, Terceira and Graciosa centre around the long sausage-shaped island of São Jorge. About 100 miles south-east of these is the largest island, São Miguel, and little Santa Maria, whilst romantic Flores and tiny Corvo are far to the north-west. Nine enchanting islands in all - and each one different.

A group of us travelled on a Waymark expedition to explore most of the islands beginning with a flight from Lisbon to Ponta Delgada on São Miguel: the largest town and one of the three administrative centres of the Azores Autonomous Region (the others are Horta on Fayal and Angra on Terceira). It is a town full of old world charm where the Portuguese influence is unmistakable - it could almost be a mini-Lisbon - full of churches and palaces flamboyantly Baroque or Manueline.

But we were anxious to explore the mysteries of this large island away from the capital. A line of ancient calderas runs along the spine of the island, separated by big bald hills like larger versions of the Scottish moors. The calderas are now water filled: deep and mysterious lakes and none more so than the Lagoa do Fogo, in the centre of the island. We climbed from the coast into a wild moorland scene and from the tops could see small volcanic cones, erupting like pimples on the plains below, proving, if proof were needed, the volcanic origins of the island. Another dramatic volcanic landscape was that around the romantic Sete Cidades, a village with two lakes, the Lago Azul and Lago Verde, and there was no mistaking which was which for one was bright blue and the other bright green! We walked a high narrow ridge round the lakes and could see the ocean on either hand until at last we descended to the village in time to catch the bus back to Ponta Delgada.

A few days later we visited Furnas, a charming little town set in a bowl of wooded hills at the eastern end of the island, where in the 18th century Thomas Hickling, an English entrepreneur, built a fine Georgian house with superb gardens called Terra Nostra Park, now open to the public. Exotic trees and plants thrive here because warm water flows in the streams - the town earns its name from the many fumaroles and boiling springs in the area. The whiff of sulphur is never far away and one would suspect the Devil of having a hand in this place, but for the fact that it is more like Heaven than Hell. Up above the town, in idyllic landscape, is the Furnas Lake, with its own solfataras where the locals cook *cozido* in hermetically sealed pots, dropped into the sizzling hot holes.

It really is quite surprising to discover how far apart some of these islands are. It took us one and a half hours to fly from São Miguel to Flores - all the islands except Corvo have an airport - and to be greeted by a baggage roundel scarcely bigger than a large dining table. The island's capital, Santa Cruz, is a scattered collection of nondescript buildings and not a prepossessing sort of place but as we explored the island over the next couple of days we all fell in love with Flores itself. In early summer it lives up to its name, with vivid blue hedgerows of hydrangea, along with banks of double red roses, wild clematis intertwining higher trees and great mop-heads of deep blue agapanthus. For two days we walked the steep coast from Lajedo to Ponta Delgada (another one!) clambering past landslips and fording the rushing Fajazinha River. It was two days of excitement with no guarantee of getting through to the end - the locals said we'd never make it - though we did. The scenery was stunning and in my opinion this is one of the finest coastal walks I have ever been on. From the cliffs above Fajazinha the Ribeira Grande waterfall plunged in a thousand foot drop, whilst out to sea little Corvo island lay like a battleship at anchor. Just off the coast was the rock of Monchique - the westernmost piece of Europe!

At Flores in the Azores Sir Richard Grenville lay, says Tennyson in his epic poem, *The Revenge.* And the sea we gazed upon from these cliffs was the very place where in 1591 Sir Richard Grenville of the Revenge fought one of the great naval encounters of all time. The Revenge, with 190 men, fought hand-to-hand against fifteen Spanish ships and five thousand men for fifteen hours before finally being overcome. *God of battles, was ever a battle like this in the world before?* Grenville was captured but died of his wounds a few days later.

We flew then to Horta in Fayal, a very different sort of island, world renowned as a calling place for intrepid round-the-world sailors, who paint their insignia on the harbour walls. Judging from the results, which make

This coastal path above Fajã dos Vimes was until recently the only way into the village. These isolated coastal strips (fajãs) on São Jorge in the Azores are now accessible by road

Horta harbour resemble an outdoor art gallery, there's a lot of people sailing round the world! Everyone calls at the little bar which is Peter's Cafe Sport down by the harbour, if only to buy the prestigious T-shirt, which, like that from Phantom Ranch in the depths of Grand Canyon, can't be obtained anywhere else.

When clipper flying boats crossed the Atlantic, Horta was their port of call but that finished with the war. The island still played an important part in communications until fairly recently, however, because the transatlantic cables came this way. Now the cables like the clippers are part of history, replaced by satellites, and their old staff quarters are incorporated into the Fayal Hotel.

Any doubts about the volcanic nature of the Azores is quickly dispelled by a visit to Ponta dos Capelinhos across the island from Horta. Here, in 1957-8 a new island rose from the sea in a welter of hissing steam and flying cinders. It quickly joined the 'mainland' and now forms a huge cape of steepsided ash. A lighthouse and several cottages were destroyed in the holocaust and the emergence and growth of the volcanic monster is shown in a small museum nearby. We climbed the remnant ash cone in a half gale of wind and rain, noticing how the slopes were littered with those round volcanic stones called bombs, thrown out by the volcano in eruption. It was a wild scene from the top, like Hell frozen over.

Fayal is dominated by the adjacent island of Pico, barely half an hour away by ferry. Pico means 'peak' and is the name of a mountain as well as the island, a symmetrical cone like a model of Fujiyama, 2351m high (7,714ft), by far the highest in the islands, and as a matter of fact the highest in Portugal. It is an easy if laborious ascent.

We left Fayal in a squall. The ferry boat from Horta to São Jorge ploughed through a heavy sea under leaden skies. It called at Madalena and San Roque on Pico to load and unload cargo and passengers. At San Roque the harbour leaves a lot to be desired - the passengers had to jump from the quay onto the heaving deck of the boat and I wondered how an elderly nun would manage, but she just lifted her skirts and made a nimble leap! The voyage took a little over two hours, but nobody was sorry when it was over.Under brightening skies we sailed into Velas, the island's capital and the most charming little town in the Azores.

Velas is compact, neatly clustered round the harbour and protected by tall cliffs. From the harbour the old city gates give access to a town of winding streets, a town square, historic churches and old town hall. There's a couple of good restaurants. The road above the town gives an almost aerial picture as it starts its steep descent; like looking down on Toytown.

The island itself is long and thin - 56km one way but only 8km the other. It offers superb coastal walks, comparable with those on Flores; visiting the remote *fajãs* or coastal strips with their tiny hamlets. One walk took us from the Fajã dos Vimes to the Fajã de São João along the staggeringly lovely south coast. It followed an ancient track which, like all these coastal tracks, was at one time the only means of access to the remote hamlets and then only on foot or by mule. Nowadays money from the EEC has paid for new roads over the hill tops, leaving the coastal hugging tracks for the benefit of walkers. A bridge had gone on this walk involving a bit of a scramble, and in one place sweeps of scree had destroyed the path and we had to pick our way across with the utmost care, though it wasn't as tricky as the Flores coastal walk. The highlight was a beautiful waterfall and below it, hidden in the lush undergrowth, the ruins of an old corn mill.

Once again the volcanic nature of the Azores is emphasised on this island - at Urzelina there's the top half of a church tower sticking out of the ground - the rest of the church was buried by lava in 1808!

São Jorge was the last of our islands. We had gone to the Azores wondering what they were all about and had discovered an unspoilt group of islands where the pace of life is the perfect antidote for today's stresses.

7
Gorges and Canyons

There is always something particularly exciting about a deep gorge. Often they are no more than a few metres wide, with walls rising sheer for hundreds of metres and perhaps a rushing torrent below, but sometimes they are designed on an altogether bigger scale, like the Grand Canyon, which is 250 miles long and a mile deep. They exist in most mountain regions. In Britain the best known gorge is Cheddar Gorge, readily accessible by car, but there are plenty of smaller examples, especially in the limestone of the Yorkshire Dales and the Peak District. Tilberthwaite Gill near Coniston in the Lake District is more unusual. This narrow cleft is only accessible nowadays by the hardened scrambler, who has to negotiate a tricky waterfall, but in Victorian times (and for much later) it was criss-crossed by narrow wooden bridges and catwalks, allowing the visitor to penetrate into the very heart of the gorge. There are several similar gorges to this in the Alps, all quite short. They stem from the romantic era of tourism - not so romantic, however, that the proprietor didn't charge for admittance! Some still do. Well known ones include the Gorner Gorge, which starts near the Furi téléphérique station above Zermatt, and the Gorges of Diosaz at Servoz near Chamonix.

In a gorge, no matter how easy it may be, there is always a sense of being trapped and this adds an extra frisson of excitement. The danger is usually more apparent than real. There might be some slight danger of falling rocks and in some gorges there can be danger from flash floods but warning notices are generally displayed and if the warnings are heeded there is little real danger.

Some gorges, like the Virgin River described later, require wading and in such cases all vital gear should be wrapped in plastic bags. A towel can be useful, too, and this also must be protected in a plastic bag to keep it dry.

It can be incredibly hot in the confines of a gorge (the Grand Canyon soars to well over 100°F) and water becomes essential. Though the gorge may have a river or rushing stream, the chances are that the water will be undrinkable or inaccessible. A large, well filled water bottle is vital; preferably laced with Isostar.

Most gorges can be rough going at times, but there are some which require experience of scrambling to negotiate them safely. One such is the famous Torrente de Pareis on the north coast of Majorca which is some 6km long,

In the Pareis Gorge, Majorca. It takes about four hours to descend the gorge and some scrambling skill is needed

descends about 500m to the lovely bay at Sa Calobra and takes about 4 hours to descend. It is arduous - some climbing or scrambling skill is necessary and there are likely to be deep pools as well.

Exploring an unknown gorge can be hazardous; good scrambling ability and a decent length of climbing rope may prove essential, though the chief requirement is experience of such places. It is too easy to get into an irreversible situation and find yourself hopelessly stuck. In a remote area this could be fatal. *Never make a move you cannot reverse.*

A friend and I were once descending a virtually unknown gorge in the Ticino Alps, Switzerland. It seemed like a good ending to our day's walk, but as we descended it became ever more difficult and, in truth, we should have beaten a retreat, but we were both experienced climbers and scramblers and we were well committed to our chosen route. To go back would have taken us hours and we were fairly tired by this time. All the classic ingredients of a mountain accident were coming together and we should have recognized that fact.

My friend was descending a slab by a waterfall when he slipped and went crashing down some ten metres onto a shrubby ledge. But for the ledge he would have fallen much further with fatal results and though the shrubs lessened the impact of his fall he still managed to dislocate his elbow and lose his glasses, without which he was blind as a bat. I climbed down to him and tried to put the elbow back but without success, nor could I find his glasses.

Our situation was awesome. A deep gorge, a roaring waterfall and, because of the shrubs and trees in the gorge, totally hidden from the outside world. The day was advancing and it was obvious we would have to sit out the night on the ledge. We had no food (a serious mistake and we should have known better) but at least the stream was crystal clear so we didn't go thirsty. Also, because Ticino is one of the warmest parts of the Alps, the night wasn't cold so hypothermia wasn't a problem.

With his bad arm and useless sight it was obvious that my companion would have to be rescued. There was no way he could get out of the gorge on his own. So early next morning I set off back up the gorge. Only then did I fully realise what we had descended because the way back up was a tough scramble, easily Grade III by British standards. Because I had done a lot of climbing I didn't find it too difficult - in fact, at one point I paused on a ledge to stuff my mouth full of delicious bilberries. I was starving!

At last I got out of the gorge and found a path which led to the nearest village. I came across a kindly local who took me the last few miles in his car and then helped me call out the rescue services. In no time at all a helicopter came whirring over, picked me up and off we went to find the injured man. Looking down into the gorge it was impossible to see anything for the trees and it took some time, and several passes, to pick up the victim. But eventually he was winched up and we all zoomed off to the hospital in Locarno where he stayed for a couple of days while they fixed him up.

Had we not been so experienced in the mountains perhaps we would never have tackled the gorge in the first place - it was a last minute decision made when we were getting tired and our judgement was impaired. So we had no rope, no spare food, no spare glasses (which should have been carried in the rucksack) and the victim had no insurance! Rescue is not free in the Alps and his helicopter ride and hospitalization cost him £2500. Fortunately, he could afford it.

Take heed of this story and learn the lessons the inexpensive way!

As if the gorges themselves could not provide sufficient adventure, man has adapted them for his own activities. Quite apart from climbing on steep walls like those at Verdon in France, there is canyoneering, which involves wearing wet suits and sliding down waterfalls, plunging into deep pools and from time to time abseiling in an exciting descent of a narrow gorge, and there is also what seems to me the ultimate crazy thrill, bungy-jumping. In this a special elastic cord is fastened round the ankles and a dive taken from a high bridge over a canyon, so the effect is like a human yo-yo. They tell me it is exciting, but I'll take their word for it. I mention these activities here because both are offered on various adventure treks, just as white water rafting and jet boating are (see Ch 5). No training is necessary, though obviously expert guidance is required for all of them.

If you want to try all these scary activities in one concentrated package, then the place to go is Queenstown, in New Zealand's South Island. The place itself is a holiday resort on the shores of Lake Wakatipu, easily reached by air or road from Christchurch, but it has become a centre for everything that is extreme in outdoor activities. They invented bungy-jumping here and jet-boating too; every other shop in town seems devoted to outdoor sports. Climbing, white water rafting, parapenting, water skiing (and snow skiing in season) - you name it and they'll lay on an afternoon's crash course for you. Though perhaps that's not the right phrase under the circumstances!

Short Trips

The old Victorian gorge walks were all designed to be done in a day, often just an hour or two as the highlight of a longer walk. There are plenty of more exciting gorge walks which also take just a day. One of the best known is the Samaria Gorge in Crete which begins at Xyloskalon and ends on the coast at New Agia Roumeli, 18km and 5 hours later. It descends about 1200m, steeply for the first hour, then more gradually. The mid-point is the ruined village of Samaria itself after which the gorge starts to narrow until it reaches the Iron Gates where the walls are only 3m apart and soar up menacingly,

The steep start is protected with handrails and the trail is on the whole well maintained, and very popular. It is open only during the summer months when the gorge may be more or less dry whereas in winter it can be impassable. To assuage the heat of the summer months there are five water points for travellers in the gorge. Once at the coast it is usual to take a boat to Loutro, Chora Sfakion (several a day) or less frequently to Sougia and Paleohora. Alternatively it is possible to walk out to Anopoli, or of course, back up the gorge, which takes about 7 hours.

Another short but popular gorge in Europe is Corsica's Spelunca Gorge which connects the villages of Ota and Evisa in the wild country north of Ajaccio. From Ota a narrow path leads down to the Porto River and the D124 at a road bridge where the gorges proper begin. There are actually several gorges but the main one is unmistakable because the path is good, having once been the major route of communication between the two villages. At first the going is easy, rising and falling a little, with the typical pink Corsican granite soaring overhead. Remnants of paving remain from the old days and through the trees glimpses of crags and spires can be seen as the gorge penetrates the hillsides. It isn't very narrow at this point but it is very attractive and before long it plunges down steeply to a river and an ancient arched stone bridge.

Beyond the bridge the climb begins in earnest, the path zig-zagging endlessly. At first there are sensational views all round but before long trees block the view and there is nothing to take your mind off the arduous ascent except the clumps of hellebores, the rock-roses and carpets of cyclamen. If the weather is cool it's not too bad, but in the heat of the Corsican summer it requires stamina. However, before long the path emerges on the main road just outside Evisa, where there are some welcome bars! Spelunca takes between 3 and 4 hours and is an easy introduction to gorge-walking - especially as you can do it in reverse, that is by going *down* from Evisa. That takes about $2^{1}/_{2}$ hours between the villages, but it is a knee-jarring experience and some people find it more arduous.

An interesting and unusual gorge walk is that of the Virgin River Narrows in the Zion National Park, Utah, USA. It is probably unique in that it follows the actual river bed - in fact it could do little else because the river fills the narrow cleft from side to side. The sandstone walls are only 15m apart and rise sheer for 600m on either hand.

At first the river, which is gentle flowing, is no more than ankle deep but suddenly it gets very much deeper - chest high in some seasons - and you can see walkers struggling to keep their rucksacks and cameras clear of the water. The deep bit is only 20 or 30 metres long, then it becomes shallow again. Here and there it is possible to climb out of the water onto a shingle bank, but somehow there is always a sense of menace about this walk - perhaps because there is the incipient threat of a flash flood. Such floods *do* occur, especially in spring when the melt water is coming down off the high ground. The park rangers post warnings at the entrance to the gorge at times of potential danger. They say you can hear the rumble of a flash flood approaching, but there's nothing you can do about it. It must be terrifying.

The Virgin River walk can be continued for some 25 miles but most visitors just walk upstream for an hour or two before turning back. Truth to tell, after the first couple of miles it gets a bit boring.

Europe's Grand Canyon

There are many gorges in southern France and they can all be linked into a continuous trail lasting 26 days from Grasse to Langogne. (see *Walking the French Gorges* by Alan Castle. Cicerone). This includes the Verdon Gorge, but the Verdon can be done on its own as a day walk, perhaps combined with more general walking in the area. The Gorge (Grand Canyon du Verdon) makes an excellent day's walk.

The Verdon River flows down from the Sestrier Alps through the limestone heart of Provence. Below the little town of Castellane it enters a 20 mile gorge which in places is 700m deep and sometimes only 10m wide. In recent years it has become one of the world's great rock-climbing centres, but it also offers several fine walks-cum-scrambles. The best of these is the Sentier Martel, named after the celebrated cave explorer who was the first to traverse the gorge. It follows the gorge from the footbridge at l'Estellie to the Point Sublime (or vice versa, of course) and takes about 7 hours. A start can be made from the French Alpine Club hut, La Chalet Maline, or from the hotel at Les Cavaliers, perched dramatically on the opposite lip of the chasm. In either case a steep descent has to be made to reach the river and Sentier Martel.

I descended from Les Cavaliers with some companions from Headwater Holidays. We found a good path along the true right bank of the river, sometimes by the water's edge, sometimes high above it. It climbed and dipped incessantly, so the going proved fairly tough, especially as the close confines of the gorge made the atmosphere sultry. It didn't help when we found a great scree chute had swept away the path at a perilous height above the river. The scree had even obliterated some of the ladders placed to make things easier, but hand ropes had been rigged and it turned out not too difficult.

After a while we met a sign indicating the junction of the Verdon and Artuby rivers, known as La Mescla, a diversion from the main track of about half an hour, but worthwhile, for a more idyllic spot would be hard to imagine. We jogged down the twisting path to the rivers, here cool and green, and inviting for a swim on a hot day. In the clear water we could see some great fish lazily cruising back and fro and they didn't seem to mind when we joined them.

Back on the main path again, the route climbed steadily to the Brèche Imbert, a narrow col between the soaring walls of the canyon and an isolated pinnacle which stood guardian-like above the river. It was easy to climb the pinnacle and from the top we had superb views up and down the gorge. The river was far below, a silver streak.

The descent from the Brèche Imbert was by a 200m ladder - 252 rungs to be exact, and in parts very steep indeed. But there were good handrails and no sense of exposure because the rock enfolds the ladder, cutting off the downwards view - it is nothing compared with the average via ferrata in the Dolomites! (see Ch 2). There's another fine viewpoint at the foot of the ladders.

The path then climbed to a ledge high above the river before descending to the second bathing place, a little beach which is handy to the path if not as attractive as La Mescla. We should have taken a break here because a long and very tiring climb through the forests followed, leading to the tunnels. The Trescaire Tunnel, 100m long, was followed by the Tunnel du Baou, 670m long, of pitch black darkness and littered with traps for the unwary to stumble over. Windows lifted the gloom here and there (including one with ladders leading down to the river) but for the most part a torch was necessary to avoid the pitfalls. From the windows we glimpsed views of the deep and narrow Sampson Corridor, the final part of the gorge. The tunnels are a way of overcoming the passage of the Corridor, which but for them might be a bit tricky. They were built early in the century to carry water down the gorge, perhaps for some hydro-electric scheme - who knows? Originally there were seven tunnels but they are all unsafe nowadays except for the two used by the Sentier Martel.

Beyond the tunnels some steps climbed up to a car park and 20 minutes later we reached the inn at Point Sublime. And the end is also the scenic climax - the view down the gorge into the dramatic Sampson Corridor is superb. No wonder it is called Point Sublime!

The Long River - through the Gorges of the Yangtse, China

Some gorge walks take several days, like the Blyde Canyon, South Africa, and the Fish River Canyon, Namibia. Access is limited in this latter to winter only because it is too hot in summer. There are some restrictions on numbers too.

In China the gorges of the Yangtse River are world famous, especially those below Chongqing (Chungking). At 6300km the Yangtse is the third longest river in the world winding across China from Tibet to the East China Sea near Shanghai. Yangtse is its English name, more correctly rendered in modern Pinyin as Yangzi, but the old form is much preferred, and in any case the Chinese name for the river is Ch'ang Jiang - *the long river* - which shows how sensible the Chinese are in these matters.

There are luxury tourist boats sailing the river but some years ago I travelled on a normal ferry from Yiling to Chongqing. We had a small and smelly cabin, but the rest of the boat was crowded, with people sleeping on the decks. We started in the middle of the night and at dawn next day were sailing through the first of the great gorges, the Xiling Gorge, which is 80km long. The swiftly flowing river sometimes seemed to send the boat backwards because we were beating against the current. The water was the colour of milk chocolate. It was summer and at a high level but it can fall 30m in the winter. Fallen logs floated down and not just logs - two bloated bodies floated past as well.

The Wu Gorge came next, 40km long, squeezed between cliffs 900m high in which were cut long walkways for the trackers, whose job it was in the old days to tow the boats upstream against the current. A large boat needed hundreds of trackers. There are still a few small boats pulled this way, though we did not see any. All the small boats, mostly sampans, were going downstream at a furious rate of knots, carried by the swirling current. I traced the path for miles through the cliffs, thinking what a splendid trek it would make, though I have not heard of anyone doing it. The Chinese have a plan to flood the gorges

The Jade Dragon Snow Mountains above Lijiang in Yunnan.
The Tiger Leaping Gorge cuts deeply through these peaks

in a vast hydro-electricity project, so perhaps these venerable walkways will be lost forever.

The first port of call was the town of Badong; large modern buildings piled up on the riverside and looking curiously like the Potala at Lhasa. Crowds milled on the jetty and an immense flight of steps led up into the town. Every so often the boat passed smaller hamlets and sometimes cross-river ferries. The third gorge, the Qutang, is a mere 8km but the river is narrow and the stream at its most violent. Buoys marked our course and the boat obediently zig-zagged up the river, propellers thrashing like mad against the strong current.

In the forward lounge that evening most people read or talked though some managed to play chess watched by a critical audience. The river buoys became pinpricks of light - green for starboard, red for port - as the boat continued through the dark night.

Early next morning we came to Wanxian and went ashore, climbing steps like something out of Potemkin up into the town and watching the activity of the street markets. It is a most attractive town, with lots going on. Beyond

Wanxian the river widened and became more pastoral until at last we chugged into Chongqing after a memorable boat journey.

Three thousand miles to the west the river rises in Tibet and flows in an enormous S-bend through the state of Yunnan. Here the Yangtze is known as the Jinsha Jiang (*the river of golden sand*) though it is hard to imagine why. Far from golden sands the river cuts through a series of enormous gorges, and one of these, the Tiger Leaping Gorge, is an exciting walk. The trip starts in the town of Lijiang which has a marvellous skyline of mountains - the Jade Dragon Snow Mountain, which resembles the aiguilles above Chamonix. We were sorry to leave Lijiang, for it is one of the prettiest towns in Yunnan, and the home of Naxi culture, not to mention Mama Fu's, where you get some of the best egg-and-chips in China. But as the old bus pulled laboriously over a zig-zag pass we looked forward to the Tiger Leaping Gorge. It is only in the last few years that the Chinese have opened these remote regions to foreigners, and we were fortunate in being with Explore Worldwide on their inaugural trip to Yunnan. The road, such as it was, ran alongside the Yangtze to the little town of Qiaotou, where the walk was to begin. Not to be outdone, however, the bus driver took us about half a mile up the track, which was rocky enough to gladden the heart of any 4WD driver. The road was narrow and the river boiled over rocks a hundred feet below. We were glad to get out and walk.

The gorge began without any preamble; a precipitous gap squeezed between the Jade Dragon Snow Mountain on the one hand and the Haba Mountains on the other. We were following the flow of the river as we walked along the good path, so though there were ups and downs on the way, the overall course was down - from 6820ft at Qiaotou to 6360ft at Walnut Grove, the romantically named but fairly grotty hamlet where we spent the first night. It is about halfway through the gorge and took us 6 hours' walking to reach.

As we strolled along we tried to comprehend the scale of the gorge. The river was far below - one hundred, two hundred feet, who knows? But across the river on the Jade Dragon Snow Mountain flank rose the most savage cliffs and pinnacles I have ever seen. Imagine the Chamonix aiguilles piled one on top of another in a gigantic stack of spires and you get the idea. From the river to the top of the crags is a staggering 11,700ft (3900m); equivalent to two Eigerwands, one on top of another, or two and a half times the height of Ben Nevis.

The rest house bed at Walnut Grove was hard so I was not reluctant to make an early start next morning. The great gorge continued, though now the path narrowed in places, giving more exposure. After a couple of hours the gorge started to widen and the path climbed suddenly and steeply to the village of Youan, perched on the edge of a fertile plateau where the workers were gathering the wheat harvest. Beyond the plateau the path dropped in sharp zig-zags to the river and the motorised punt which acted as a ferry.

Once over the river we climbed steeply to another plateau and walked to the village of Daju, and a nice guesthouse known as the Tiger Leaping Gorge Hotel. After lunch I walked round the village, which is surrounded by high mountains. A breeze was blowing through the gorge and stirring up the dusty earth in dancing eddies. I know now why the Chinese spit so much - it is to clear the dust from their throats. But the breeze no doubt helped the women who were busy winnowing, the chaff blowing away from the winnowing baskets in little flurries. The old houses and their courtyards were very attractive, the land separated sometimes by prickly pear hedges. In the fields below the village the locals were working to bring in the harvest and the whole scene presented a picture of ageless, enduring, China.

Daju was the end of the Tiger Leaping Gorge, but we were not finished with the Yangtze. Beyond the Tiger Leaping Gorge the river made a gigantic bend cut off from the world by high hills. In the bend there was a village called Baoshan (a common name in Yunnan), virtually unknown to western travellers, and it was our plan to visit it. So we piled into the bus again and made a heart-stopping drive over a precipitate pass to the hamlet of Gole (7550ft), the start of the Baoshan trek.

We picked up porters here, including an incredibly cheery bunch of young girls. I watched a tiny slip of a lass pick up my heavy Karrimor Sequoia and, ignoring the straps, tie it to her basket with string. Then she added another! As we climbed the steep ridge above the village I panted and puffed but the girls kept up a non-stop chattering and giggling which kept us all in good spirits. The ridge was at least a thousand feet and when at last we reached the top there were wonderful views over the bend in the Yangtze and distant mountain ranges.

The path descended steeply into a little valley. It was badly eroded with channels shoulder deep in places, like trenches from the first world war. People had been walking this way for thousands of years.

The valley seemed very fertile and a couple of distant hamlets appeared, then we saw Baoshan, perched like Shangri La on an outcrop of rock. It was impressive and moving; the deep bend of the river, the little village isolated above it. The number of westerners who had seen this sight before could be counted on the fingers of one hand.

Baoshan was a warren of steep streets and steps, hugging its rock. The people were friendly, courteous and though some displayed natural curiosity, they were never intrusive. We ate our noodles in a courtyard and I slept the night in a bean store listening to the scratching of the resident mouse.

Next day we followed our porters out of the village and out of the valley, climbing another ridge to the village of Yangsi Lak. This time there were no chattering girls; all the porters were men and they carried just one bag each. It was steep, arduous work, a relentless 7 hours of toil. Slowly the valley below

*Shangri-la! The virtually unknown hamlet of Baoshan above the
Yangtze gorge in Yunnan*

disappeared from sight. Baoshan might never have been. Shangri La was
gone.

I have thought ever since what a marvellously exciting adventure it would
be to connect the two halves of this walk by continuing from Youan round the
great bend of the Yangtze to reach Baoshan. Whether it can be done I have no
idea.

One Mile Down, One Mile Up - Across the Grand Canyon, USA

No account of gorges would be complete without mentioning the greatest
of them all, the Grand Canyon of the Colorado River in Arizona.
"Whoever stands upon the brink of the Grand Canyon beholds a spectacle
unrivalled on this earth", said the geologist F.E. Mattheson, pointing out that
no other gorge could match it for "its vastness, its majesty, its ornate sculpture
and its wealth of colour." It follows a winding course from the Marble Gorge
to the Grand Wash cliffs of about 280 miles and it varies in width from 4 to 18
miles and is about a mile deep. The finest part of the gorge, 56 miles long, has

been declared a national park, with two major centres, on the North Rim and South Rim respectively.

So vast is this canyon that there are lesser gorges within it - each of which would be a major gorge elsewhere. Bands of different rock reveal half the world's geological time; sandstones, shales, limestones and schists, right down to the Zoroaster granite bedrock - two billion years.

Most tourists go to the South Rim Visitor Centre, which has now grown into a large complex called Grand Canyon Village with its own airfield and even its own steam trains (a 65 mile journey to the town of Williams). The village and its campsite are open all year. On the other hand the North Rim centre is only open for the summer months because the North Rim is 300m higher than the South Rim and gets 355mm of snow, making access difficult and descent to the Canyon virtually impossible.

There are 11 trails in and across the Canyon, nine starting at the South Rim and two at the North Rim. The longest is the 72 mile Tonto Trail, along the Canyon from Garnet Canyon to Red Canyon, but the most popular trails are the Bright Angel Trail from South Rim down to the river and the corresponding North Kaibab Trail from North Rim to the river. They meet at Bright Angel Campground and so it is possible to combine the two to make a crossing of the Canyon, usually from north to south. Grand Canyon is about 17 miles wide at this point but the two trails add up to about $23^1/2$ miles, with 5840ft of descent and 4400ft of ascent. The tracks are good but the heat is fierce and it is usual to camp twice en route. Some of the signs are pretty blunt: one says *If you try to reach the Colorado River and back in a day, you will die.*

You certainly need lots of water - a half gallon, which should be filled at every scarce water point. In a recent three year period 750 hikers have had to be rescued, mostly due to dehydration.

On the other hand it is so warm that a sleeping bag and tent are quite unnecessary. You do have to carry food and cooking utensils, of course, including a stove. No trash can be buried or burned, it has all to be carried out - the rangers are keen on that, and on the permit to overnight in the Canyon, obtainable free from the visitor centres.

When I crossed the Canyon my companions and I inadvertently chose the hottest days of the year. In Death Valley a few days earlier the temperature had reached 109°F (43°C), but on our second day in the Canyon it reached 120°F (49°C). Believe me, that's hot!

A few spectators saw us start off from the North Rim with our large rucksacks and cheered us on the way with whooping 'yahoos' as if we were the 7th Cavalry going into action. It was a steep descent and we passed several groups of mules, sure footed and stately slow, led by a teamster. Mule trains descend from both South and North rims to Phantom Ranch, a rest house near the Colorado River, and go back the way they came. The track was so narrow we had to press back into the rock out of harm's way, as the mules stepped delicately on the very edge of an abysmal drop. The riders looked rigid with fright, and who can blame them. François Matthes, a surveyor who improved the trail in 1902, said it was so steep his mules just slid down on their haunches!

As the path zigzagged down the scenery grew ever more magnificent with great ribs of red rock plunging into deep gorges and a waterfall spouting from a cliff opposite the track. After a while we came to Bruce's Farm, a low building just off the track where Bruce Aiken lives, an artist who paints pictures of the canyon

A steep descent near the top of Bright Angel Trail, Grand Canyon

and sells them in various galleries at high prices. Bruce provided us with delicious free lemonade; a more than welcome thirst quencher, gulped down like legionnaires lost in the desert.

Just beyond Bruce's Farm the Canyon opens out as Roaring Springs Canyon meets Bright Angel Canyon and the going levels out. Before long we came to Cottonwood Campground, a place of basic facilities but, like all the national park campgrounds, immaculately kept by the Rangers. We had come a mere 7 miles from the rim, but it seemed three times that.

After a meal, we prepared to sleep and hung our rucksacks from a pole for safety's sake. There are no bears as there are in Yosemite, but there are coyotes, racoons and squirrels, all prepared to attack a rucksack in search of goodies. I rolled my camping mat out near a patch of scrub and as I was dozing off heard the unmistakable whirring of a rattlesnake in the bushes. But I was too tired to care, and in any case most snakes won't bother you if you don't bother them.

Next morning we were away bright and early, at first treading an easy path then making a diversion to see the well-named Ribbon Falls which spray down into a little side canyon. This caused us some trouble with the Bright Angel Creek but eventually we were able to enter the deep black slot of Box Canyon. The high walls of this gorge keep out the sun so the walking was pleasantly cool, along a good and almost level path. The magnificence of the surroundings defies imagination; it was like being in some great natural cathedral. Here we were almost at the bottom of the Canyon - twelve geological time zones deep, two billion years, or half the Earth's lifetime.

But as we stepped out of Box Canyon the sun struck us with the searing heat of a blast furnace. We staggered on to reach the cabins of Phantom Ranch where there was shade and a cold beer. The 'ranch' was built in 1922 as a place where tourists could stay after riding down on mules, usually from South Rim. It is booked up well in advance. For those less fortunate, the Bright Angel Campground is nearby.

We met a Ranger at the Ranch who warned us that the day was going to get even hotter and that it was already the hottest day of the year so far - a sizzling 47°C (116°F) at the Ranch and 4° higher on the trail. He recommended we wait until things cooled down a bit but our leader, Jeff, wanted to press on so that we could see the sunset from the Tonto Plateau which was some distance up the path to the South Rim. It was a tactical error.

At first all went well. We soon reached the Silver Bridge over the Colorado, a swiftly flowing, grey stream, reduced to a shadow of its former tumultuous self by the building of the Glen Canyon Dam upstream in 1965. There are still cataracts, however, and rafting on the Colorado is very popular - it was here that river rafting began as a sport. Earlier still, in 1869, John Wesley Powell and nine companions took four flimsy wooden boats for a thousand miles along the raging Colorado in one of the great epics of exploration.

Beyond the river we started the climb up the Bright Angel Trail towards the South Rim. The sun was burning in its intensity and a couple of people dropped out for a breather. Soon the trail began a series of long, exhausting zig-zags known as the Devil's Corkscrew, which brought us to our knees. The fitter members forged ahead, doggedly, the weaker souls dropped back. Water was at a premium - a half gallon seemed to last no time at all.

My legs felt like lead and halfway up the Corkscrew I just collapsed in the shade of a rock. Some girl hikers, on their way down the trail, generously filled my water bottle, since they would soon be at Phantom Ranch. I staggered a bit further, but the heat of the day grew even fiercer, and I looked for somewhere to hide.

At last I found a slight cave and crawled inside for a couple of hours. Fortunately there were some spectacular views. Down in the Canyon the Devil's Corkscrew looked like a ribbon tossed by a careless child, whilst all around rose the multi-coloured mesas and banded walls of the Canyon. When eventually the day began to cool I made my way up to the Indian Gardens Campground; a place of shady trees and kleptomaniac chipmunks.

That night was one of the most moving I can remember. The black walls of the Canyon soared up to meet a deep purple night sky, with millions of bright stars spread like diamonds on a carpet. Tired though I was I didn't want to go to sleep - just to gaze at the wonderful heavens.

Next morning we were away early to avoid the heat of the day. The path still climbed severely, but now there were regular water points and the great cliffs of the South Rim offered shade for quite a time. I could see the fierce light playing on the very tops but on the trail it was still relatively cool. By 9 am the trail had become a caravan route busy with mule trains and day hikers but the Rim was near and I felt a growing sense of achievement and excitement. I'd crossed the Grand Canyon!

Two of us breasted the South Rim together. An elderly matron watched us and our great packs in wonder. At last she said, "Have you guys come from the *North Rim* ?" We agreed we had. "Gee, let me buy you a beer," she said. "That's some damned hike!"

Appendix 1
Special Interests

There is no reason why an adventure holiday should not be slanted towards a particular interest, whether it be flowers, bird life, archaeology or one of the many other passions people have these days. There are firms who specialise in such trips, but remember also that many general adventure trips will include various interests as well; for example it is scarcely possible to follow one of the Alpine trails in June without being almost overwhelmed by the variety of flora. I remember a field outside Contamines, below Mont Blanc, which was a riot of colour and on another occasion walking up to the Col de la Vanoise to find it covered in a blue carpet of gentians. In late spring the valleys of Corsica are filled with pale hellebores, bright cistus shrubs and the tall asphodel. In more exotic locations I have come across gorgeous rhododendrons the size of cabbages in Yunnan and on the slopes of Mount Kinabalu. Sometimes such discoveries are touchingly breathtaking - how can I ever forget a single deep purple iris I came across in the deserts of Jordan for example? Specialised *Plant-hunting* trips are organised by the Alpine Garden Society and the Field Studies Council Overseas, amongst others. Here are some specialist tour operators:

Alpine Flowers, Domaine de Mansen, 32230 Louslitges, France (33.62-70-96-56)

Camp One (Himalayan Adventures Ltd), Unit 7, Enterprise House, Bridge Street, Bedale, North Yorks DL8 2AD (01677 426114)

Director of Tours, AGS, 19, Polstead Road, Oxford OX2 6TW (01865 516100)

FSC Overseas (UAG), Montford Bridge, Shrewsbury SY4 1HW (01743 850164)

Greentours Natural History Holidays, The Lodge, Cargate Lane, Saxlingham Thorpe, Norwich NR15 ITU (01508 471353)

Naturetrek, Chautara, Bighton, Nr Alresford, Hants SO24 9RB (01962 733051)

Tony Titchen, 29 Nore Road, Bristol BS20 9HN (01275 848629)

For those who prefer watching birds or animals there are many excursions to bird sanctuaries and game reserves, such as Bharatpur in India or the Kruger National Park in South Africa. *Discover the World, The Flatt Lodge, Bewcastle, near Carlisle CA6 6PH (01737 218801)* even offer whale watching! Others offering birdwatching include:

Gambia Experience, Kingfisher House, Rownhams Lane, North Baddesley, Hants SO52 9LP (01703 730888)

Naturetrek, Chautara, Bighton, Nr Alresford, Hants SO20 9RB (01962 733051)

Wildlife Worldwide, 170 Selsdon Road, South Croydon, Surrey CR2 6PJ (0181 667 9158)

A rather different sort of adventure is to embark on a pilgrimage. Most famous is the Way of St James, the walk to Compostella in Spain. There are several alternative starting points, but the usual one is Le Puy in France. It is a long walk - almost a thousand miles - and a friend of mine who did it a couple of years ago took three months over it. Several firms tackle it on a different basis, motoring a lot of the distance, to cut down the time required but purists probably regard this as cheating! One firm specialising in pilrimages is *Tangney Tours, Pilgrim House, Station Court, Borough Green, Kent TN15 8AF (01732 886666)*

Another sort of adventure can be had by tracing the campaigns of various wars. Increasingly popular, these range from simple excursions like walking Waterloo (the battlefield, not the station!) to tougher trips following the Peninsula War across the Pyrenees or even more recent events like the Vietnam campaign. Two firms specialising in this are:

Holts' Tours, 15 Market Street, Sandwich, Kent CT13 9DA (01304 612248)

Midas Battlefield Tours, The Old Dairy, The Green, Godstone, Surrey RH9 8DY (01883 744955)

Of course, not all the special tours are adventure holidays - some could rightly be classed as activity holidays where the aim is to learn painting or drama or what have you.

Finally mention must be made of some firms who specialise in just a single country. I think the doyen of these must be Dick Phillips who has been doing adventurous trips to Iceland for as long as most of us can remember: *Dick Phillips, Whitehall House, Nenthead, Alston, Cumbria CA3 3PL (01434 381440)*. For those who are looking for somewhere very different, there is Libya where two tours, one antiquities and one desert, can be done with *Arab Tours Ltd, 60 Marylebone Lane, London W1M 5FF (0171 935 3273)*

A great many firms - well over 200 - specialising in adventure travel of all kinds are members of the Association of Independent Tour Operators (AITO). Details of what they are offering can be gleaned from the AITO Directory. Copies are available from *AITO, 133a St Margaret's Road, Twickenham, Middlesex TW1 1RG (0891 515948)*.

Appendix 2
Memories are made of this...

The chances are you are on the trip of a lifetime... the chances are you will never pass this way again... so you will want something to remember it by. Even if the highlights remain in your memory for the rest of your life, the details will fade; names of erstwhile comrades will be forgotten, and places too - what *was* the name of that Dyak village? And what was the headman called? Particularly where the names are in a strange tongue, it is so easy to forget.

The most immediate answer is a daily diary and every traveller should keep one. It need not be an elaborate affair - I personally use a reporter's notebook; the flip-over kind of notebook, A5 in size and lined. In this I keep a very basic diary, sometimes illustrated by little sketches and maps (a drawing can sometimes save a lot of words!). My diary is often little more than a list of names, times, and terse impressions, but is enough to stimulate my memory when I get home. Of course, as a writer I am going to write it up properly at some time, using those elements I need for a story, whereas most people would not need to transcribe their diary and for that reason would make a fuller job of it in the first place. I once accompanied a Canadian woman who seemed to write solidly for an hour each evening. She was a teacher and used her notes in class, but even so it did seem to be overdoing it. There are often so many distractions on a trip that it needs willpower to do the diary conscientiously and sometimes, too, it is physically difficult, or you are simply too tired after an exhausting day.

Make sure you have notebook, pencils and penknife and that the book is wrapped in plastic to guard it against the weather. It's no fun trying to write on soggy paper, and incidentally, pencil is better than biro or ink because if the paper does get wet your notes will remain legible.

You need the notebook as backup even if you opt for more sophisticated note taking, such as a pocket tape recorder or a lap-top word processor. Personally I think these are fine for days out at home but they can be a bit of a nuisance on an adventure trip. You need to have plenty of tapes for the recorder and though you can get immediate impressions throughout the day, Murphy's Law dictates that you will run out of tape at a crucial moment. Most lap-tops are too heavy - and too expensive - to take on an adventure trip, though the pocket Psion organiser weighs only the same as a paperback novel, (Series 3a 512), lasts for 50 hours or so and holds 40,000 words which can be downloaded onto a desktop PC or Mac. These gizmos are probably only for the professional travel writer - but very few seem to use them.

I mentioned that I sometimes do small sketches in my notebook, but some travellers like to go a bit further and have a proper sketch pad on which to record their impressions. Force of circumstances sometimes makes this impossible but sketches have an intimacy which photographs don't seem to match. The fact that you 'can't draw' should not deter you; the very act of getting it down on paper will bring it all back vividly in years to come. The sketches can be pencil but a fine pen, like Artline, is more pleasing, though the pad needs to be protected against rain. Even watercolour sketches are possible - we are talking here of intimate little drawings just three or four inches across, which take literally minutes to do. A couple of sable brushes carried in a brush tube for protection and a small folding paintbox of limited range but good quality are all that's needed - the water comes from your water bottle. Any art shop will advise on equipment, or see David Bellamy, *The Practical Guide to Painting in the Wild*. Webb & Bower. (This is David Bellamy the artist, incidentally, not the botanist!)

Click!

For most travellers, however, photography is the chief way of recording a trip. A recent survey in an outdoor magazine revealed that a staggering 94% of readers owned a camera and of those 60% were *actively* interested in photography. The world must be awash with travel pictures! But whether they are *good* travel pictures is another matter.

On more sedate holidays the camcorder seems to have replaced the family box-brownie, but camcorders are heavy. Travelling by bus or Land Rover there may be no problem, but carrying a camcorder long distances needs dedication. No doubt camcorders will get lighter before too long.

At present the 35mm camera is favourite and it is easy to see why - there's a wide variety of models and film is readily available even in the most out of way places. Some professionals prefer larger formats which produce 6x6cm images (Bronica, Hasselblad, Rollieflex etc.) or large 'landscape' formats like 6x4.5, 6x7, or 6x9cm of which the best known is probably the Pentax 67. These are heavier, bulkier, demand more film and are very expensive (several thousand pounds in some cases). Needless to say, in the right hands they produce superb pictures and many people believe that a good big 'un will always beat a good little 'un!

There are smaller formats than 35mm and some of them can produce reasonable results, but the film is not always easy to come by and why bother when there are so many good lightweight mainstream cameras today? Having said that, I should warn you than an entirely new cartridge system has been developed recently known as APS (Advanced Photo System) which is 40% smaller than 35mm and which may eventually replace the latter. At the moment only a print film is available but transparency material is being researched and will doubtless happen before too long. APS film will not fit ordinary cameras and APS cameras (both SLR and compacts are available from all the major companies) cannot take ordinary film. Having studied this new system its advantages seem to me minimal, and certainly not worth the expense of re-equipping. I wonder if that's what the photo firms had in mind? It puts a novice in something of a quandary, though, if he or she is about to buy a camera for the first time...all of what follows applies to APS as well as 35mm.

For some time now the standard camera has been the SLR, or *single lens reflex*, so called because the viewfinder by means of a prism works through the actual camera lens. The lens is interchangeable with others of different focal lengths so you can have wide-angle shots for all-embracing views or telephoto shots for close ups. Because changing lenses can be difficult and time consuming, in some situations, a multi-purpose lens, called a zoom, was developed, covering a wide range of focal lengths. On my Nikon, for example, two zoom lenses, 28-70mm and 70-210mm, take the place of

28mm, 35mm, 50mm, 90mm, 105mm, 135mm and 200mm lenses. Obviously the saving in weight, money and time is enormous. Some photographers will tell you that a zoom is not as good as a 'prime' lens, but provided a good quality zoom is used, you really can't tell the difference. Most of the pictures in this book were taken with zooms.

I find I use the 28-70mm lens more than the other and if you are buying an SLR for the first time remember *you do not have to buy the standard 50mm lens such cameras are often sold with*. I recommend you buy a camera body plus this zoom.

Modern SLR cameras are very sophisticated. They have automatic exposure, focusing and film wind, with manual override on the exposure so that taking a picture can be as simple or technical as you wish. A UV or Skylight filter over the lens helps protect it.

In recent years the SLR itself has been under seige by the modern compact camera. As its name suggests this is light and small and in many cases can be slipped easily into a pocket. It has improved enormously in recent years with zoom lenses, auto focus and exposure and now warrants serious consideration for adventure travel. Though you cannot change the lens the zooms are fairly wide (35mm to 105mm is common, some wider still), so who needs to? The expert will probably still prefer the robustness of the SLR but a good quality compact will give excellent results. I often carry a little Minolta and some of the pictures used in this book were taken with it. Not all compacts are zooms, by the way, but zooms are preferable because of their scope.

Even a compact camera is an expensive investment and adventure travel, by its very nature, can sometimes treat them rough. The camera needs a protective case and often the one provided by the manufacturer is not robust enough, especially with compacts. I once had an almost new compact ruined in a thunderstorm because the case wasn't up to it. A good padded case, like those of Camera Care, is best. Even so, in a prolonged storm it is wise to put the camera deep in the rucksack out of harm's way! A keen photographer will no doubt have a professional camera bag with various bodies, lenses and bits and pieces, safely snug against the worst the elements can throw at it, but most travellers would not want such a cumbersome load.

The camera needs protecting against other things too. Sea air is not good for it and sea spray is death because salt corrosion can gum up the works in no time. If your camera has been in this situation wipe it carefully, inside and out, and dry it off as soon as possible. A traveller comes across other noxious fumes too, such as suphur fumes from volcanic activity, including the popular hot springs found in many parts of the world from Tuscany to Turkmenistan - and I've had suphur baths in both places.

Sand and fine grit are also deadly enemies. With reasonable care these are not likely to damage the camera itself but they *will* damage the film by scratching the surface. To avoid this, great care should be taken when reloading in dusty places - a desert being the obvious example.

Because modern cameras are battery powered they are affected by low temperatures, but quite honestly too much can be made of this. I've been in some fairly cold places but never experienced any problems. If you are expecting extreme cold, the camera can be 'winterized' by the manufacturer - at a cost. Always, but always, carry spare batteries. Auto focus compacts are particularly heavy on current.

Film

A t its best black and white photography is an art form, the lack of colour emphasising the sculptural qualities of the subject, whether it be the craggy face of an Indian holy man or the stark landscape of Death Valley in California. It is worth searching out and studying some of the great practitioners whose work appears in books, such as Frank Smythe, Walter

Poucher, Vittoria Sella or Ansel Adams. To achieve this sort of perfection takes great dedication and the final result depends as much on the time spent in the darkroom as behind the camera, so it is beyond the scope of most ordinary travellers.

Everyone takes colour shots these days - but what sort? If all you want from a trip is a nice album of pictures as a memento, then print material will be your choice, but to show slides to the local WI you obviously need slide material. It is useful to remember that print film names often end in 'color' (Fujicolor, Vericolor, Orwocolor etc.) while slide material ends in 'chrome' (Ektachrome, Fujichrome etc.). Print film is usually in 24 shot cassettes and slides in 36 shot cassettes, but in some makes either are also available in 12, 24 and 36 shots.

Because many of my pictures are for use in magazines or books I prefer to take slides or 'trannies' (transparencies) as they are called in publishing. This is the preferred medium for illustrations, though *good quality* prints can be used too. Trouble is, there's some pretty poor prints around. You can always have prints made from trannies, albeit at a cost - a decent machine print from a trannie costing roughly twice what a negative print would cost. Specialist *hand printing* is best kept for that great shot you intend to frame and hang on the study wall - it costs about four times what you pay for machine printing. Details of all these services are to be found the in various camera magazines.

Transparency film (ask for *diapositive* on the Continent) comes either process paid or not. Make sure you know which you are buying. In the end costs work out much the same, but with process paid the cost comes up front. It is the simpler method for the average traveller and some films can only be bought that way in any case. Whatever film you use you need to learn its qualities - not all film is the same by any means. I use Fujichrome because it is 'warmer' but that's a subjective judgement and any good make will serve you well. The worst thing you could do is to keep switching from one sort to another.

The film speed is important and is measured on a scale known as ISO (until fairly recently better known as ASA). The higher the ISO number the faster the film, ie. it needs less light than a lower numbered film and so can use faster shutter speeds or smaller lens apertures in any given situation. These three factors - film speed, shutter speed and aperture - are crucial in getting a correctly exposed film. (Print film will tolerate a slightly wider margin of error than slide film.) I refer you to the photo manuals if you want to know more, but fortunately modern cameras will work it all out for you under *most* conditions, which is why they are called 'automatic'. If you want to override the automatic that's up to you - but read the manual first.

I find that ISO100 is the most satisfactory speed for travel photography and virtually all the pictures in this book are on ISO100. A point to remember is that zoom lenses usually have a smaller range of apertures than prime lenses, so you often need a reasonable film speed. It depends on the situation; ISO50 or even 25 is suitable for the bright glare of India or the Sahara, whereas in gloomy jungle, like Borneo, ISO400 is not too fast. In adventure travel pictures often have to be snatched in haste, so fast film, fast shutter speeds, open apertures are the rule. If a film is too fast, however, it starts to get grainy, which is not too clever if the pictures are to be published. Perhaps you can now appreciate why the professional photographer carries his big camera bag, with several camera bodies, different film, various lenses and every device known to man for the job in hand.

Whatever film you decide to use make sure you take plenty on your adventure. If you spend two weeks trekking to Everest, taking marvellous pictures, you'll feel a right prat if you run out of film just as the great mountain appears. Work out in advance how much film you'll need - then double it!

Appendix 3

Travel Clubs & Magazines

Club officials and addresses can change - these are correct for late 1996

Birmingham & Midlands Travellers' Club (0121 356 5086/449 1979)

Bristol Travellers' Club, c/o YHA, 64 Prince Street, Bristol BS1 4HU (0117 929 4123)

The Globetrotters Club, BMC/Roving, London WC1N 3XX

Leicester World Travellers (0116 270 2308)

Nottingham World Traveller's Club, c/o YMCA, Shakespeare Street, Nottingham

STEP (Scottish Travellers Exploring the Planet) (0131 445 3394/337 2170)

Trippers, 9 Byron Place, Triangle, Clifton, Bristol BS8 1JT (0117 987 2626)

Specialist area clubs

Iceland Travel Club, PO Box 434, Harrow, Middlesex HA1 3HY

South American Explorers' Club, c/o Bradt Publications, 41 Nortoft Road, Chalfont St Peter, Bucks SL9 OLA

Magazines (M = monthly, BM = Bi-monthly, Q = quarterly)

Independent & Specialist Travel, 3 Clive House, Prospect Hill, Redditch B97 4BY (BM)

Trailfinder Magazine (issued by the well-known travel company 3 times p.a.)

Wanderlust, PO Box 1832, Windsor SL4 5YG (BM)

Traveller, Wexas Ltd, 45 Brompton Rd, London SW3 1DE (Q)

Many outdoor magazines such as *TGO* and *Outdoor Illustrated* carry adventure travel features, as do newspapers like *The Sunday Times*.

Appendix 4

Packing List for Trips

The following is a suggested list only, based on the one used by the author, but it can be adapted to suit personal needs for both men and women.

Clothes	Personal	First aid (add personal medicaments)
trousers	shaving kit	plasters
shorts	toothbrush	savlon
swimgear	toothpaste	aspirin
shirts	comb	antacid tablets
T shirts	soap	throat tablets
handkerchiefs	nail clippers	bites cream
sweater	scissors	ammonia pencil
underpants	spare specs	sunburn cream
walking socks	sun glasses	sunblock
dress socks	spec straps	lip salve
trainers	torch	insect repellent
sunhat	spare battery	Lomitol, Flagyl, Ciproxin
anorak	towel	malaria tablets
boots	bumbag	iodine tablets
spare laces	bogroll	styptic pencil
gloves		emergency food (chew bars)
gaiters		Diamox (high altitude only)

water filter
water bottle
Isostar

Technical
passport
visas
tickets air/rail
money - foriegn
money - UK
credit cards
traveller's cheques (dollars)
address card
camera
lenses
film

spare camera battery
notebook
pencil
maps
compass
guidebooks
tour correspondence
insurance
Form E111 (Europe)

Other
inner sleeping bag
outer sleeping bag
therm-a-rest (karrimat)
pillow
mosquito netting

plastic bags
mug,kfs
Easy Wash
penknife
book
trekking pole(s)
day sack
rucksack/holdall

Extra Cold Weather Gear
thermal underwear
balaclava
mitts and overmitts
duvet jacket
pile jacket

An adventure trek in Iceland - a Dick Phillips speciality

INDEX

Figures in bold indicate illustrations, f indicates the reference occurs over several following pages